WITHDRAWN

# THE NEW MACRAMÉ

**Contemporary Knotted Jewelry & Accessories**

Katie DuMont

LARK BOOKS

A Division of Sterling
Publishing Co., Inc.
New York

**CHRIS BRYANT**
*Book and jacket design,
photostyling, and production*

**EVAN BRACKEN**
*Photography*

**HEATHER SMITH
CATHARINE SUTHERLAND**
*Editorial assistance*

**VAL ANDERSON**
*Proofreader*

**HANNES CHAREN**
*Production assistance*

**ORRIN LUNDGREN**
*Illustrations*

**Library of Congress Cataloging-in-Publication Data**

DuMont, Katie.
    The new macramé : contemporary knotted jewelry and accessories /
by Katie Dumont.—1st ed.
        p.   cm.
    ISBN 1-57990-163-8
    1. Macramé patterns.   2. Jewelry making.   I. Title.
  TT840.M33D86   1999
    745.594'2—dc21                                         99-37032
                                                            CIP


10 9 8 7 6 5 4 3 2 1

First Edition

Published by Lark Books, a division of
Sterling Publishing Co., Inc.
387 Park Avenue South, New York, N.Y. 10016

© 2000, Lark Books

Distributed in Canada by Sterling Publishing,
c/o Canadian Manda Group, One Atlantic Ave., Suite 105
Toronto, Ontario, Canada M6K 3E7

Distributed in Australia by Capricorn Link (Australia) Pty Ltd., P.O.        Box
6651, Baulkham Hills, Business Centre
NSW 2153, Australia

The written instructions, photographs, designs, patterns, and projects in this
volume are intended for the personal use of the reader and may be repro-
duced for that purpose only. Any other use, especially commercial use, is
forbidden under law without written permission of the copyright holder.

Every effort has been made to ensure that all the information in this book is
accurate. However, due to differing conditions, tools, and individual skills, the
publisher cannot be responsible for any injuries, losses, and other damages
that may result from the use of the information in this book.

If you have questions or comments about this book, please contact:
Lark Books
50 College St.
Asheville, NC 28801
(828) 253-0467
Printed in Hong Kong by H&Y Printing Ltd.

ISBN 1-57990-163-8

# ACKNOWLEDGMENTS

I would like to thank Deborah Morgenthal for the opportunity, Rob Pulleyn for the motive, and Chris Byrant for the means. Thanks also to Evan Bracken for his photographic expertise and Orrin Lundgren for his illustrative assistance. For furnishing props and enthusiasm, my thanks to the fine folks at Chevron Trading Post & Bead Co., Marisande Fisher of Radiant Hemp, and Linda Rose Nall. Much appreciation to Heather Smith, Hannes Charen, Catharine Sutherland, Val Anderson, and Dana Irwin for their contributions to the production of this book. A special thank-you to Dona Z. Meilach for graciously sharing photos from her book *Macramé Accessories, Patterns and Ideas for Knotting*. My sincere gratitude to all the designers and knotters who participated in this book. In particular, I would like to acknowledge the hard work, attention to detail, and creative generosity of Elaine Lieberman and Jim Gentry. Lastly, I am grateful to Willow and Sophia for insisting upon frequent walks and, as always, guiding me to what matters.

# TABLE OF CONTENTS

# INTRODUCTION

MACRAMÉ is much easier than it looks. Said another way, it looks much harder than it is. Macramé is easier than it looks because there are only a few simple knots you need to learn. Macramé looks harder than it is because these few simple knots are varied and combined in so many different ways that it gives the impression of overwhelming complexity. The truth is macramé requires minimal skill, very little room, and no elaborate equipment or expensive materials. All you really need is some kind of cord, use of your fingers, a work surface, and a few pins to hold your work in place.

This simplicity makes macramé a great craft for kids, seniors, and anyone else (of either gender) who seeks creative expression without a huge investment of time, money, and energy.

Perhaps you're skeptical. You've flipped through the pages of this book. Sure the projects look appealing, but *easy*? And what's with some of those instructions? "Loop cord 2 around cord 1 once, then bring cord 2 back around and through the loop you just made." That doesn't exactly sound easy!

Okay, I'm going to let you in on a little secret. The hardest thing about macramé is describing how to do it. It's true! Imagine trying to teach someone how to draw a circle without being able to show him or her a picture. Well, learning to tie the basic macramé knots is as simple as drawing a circle, but it's much easier to *show* you how, than to *tell* you how. Even the most descriptive prose pales in comparison to clear visual demonstration.

So, if you're new to knotting, you'll definitely want to spend some quality-time in the Knots 101 section of this book. It's packed with visual information. Get acquainted with the basic knots and combination of knots, study the illustrations, examine the photographs, and practice making the knots. Refer to the written instructions only as a last resort, and to confirm your understanding.

To simplify the project instructions, I recommend numbering your working cords from left to right. Please keep in mind that this numbering system refers to the position of the cords and not the actual cords. When you're knotting, you're always moving the cords around, but the positions never change.

Once you get comfortable with the basics and you've made some of the projects, why not customize them using different fibers and your favorite color combinations. Add polymer clay beads or feathers and charms. Double the number of cords to make a wider choker. There are zillions of variations.

When you're confident in your knotting ability and technique, create your very own original designs, or, if you're feeling creatively-challenged, look around for some macramé moldy-oldies in vintage clothing or second-hand stores. Buy an inexpensive old belt or bag and study it; you'll actually be able to *read* the knots and tell how it was made. Disassemble it if you need to. Then copy the pattern yourself using your favorite contemporary fibers.

Macramé provides both tactile and aesthetic pleasure. There really is something quite magical about making beautiful jewelry from a ball of string. And in our hurry-up, high-tech world of "needed-it-yesterday" and "faster-is-better," there is great satisfaction in the sheer simplicity and primal nature of tying knots. I hope you will join the next generation of knotters and share in the delight of *The New Macramé*.

MACRAMÉ has evolved, in large part, thanks to missionaries and sea dogs. Early missionaries spread more than just their faith when they traveled the world. Their religious vestments and linens were frequently adorned with macramé, knotted by nuns. So, they carried the craft with them to far and remote regions. Seafaring men, too, played an important role in the history of macramé—is it any wonder, with their knowledge of knots, endless hours spent on the water, and all that rope! Mariners were truly some of the earliest prolific fiber artists. They created beautiful and intricately patterned macramé (although they prefer the more manly term *fancywork*) that was both functional and decorative. They fashioned bell pulls, lanyards, rope ladders, and all sorts of protective covers and cases, as well as footwear, hats, and belts. Credit must be given to nautical knotters for bringing macramé to so many parts of the world. By bartering their knotted wares in countries throughout the world, sailors became true macramé messengers.

The word *macramé* is derived from the old Arabic word *makrama*, which loosely translates to "big ugly wall-hanging." ***No, not really.*** Actually, the term comes from 13th century Turkey and refers to the knotted fringe that decorated towels and linens. The Spaniards learned the craft from the Moors, and spread it to southern Europe as early as the 14th century. It was a well-established art in France in the 15th century and introduced to England in the late 1600s. Macramé flourished in Italy in the 17th and 18th centuries and enjoyed tremendous popularity throughout the Victorian period, when ladies of leisure passed the time by creating fancy fringes and all types of knotted embellishments. It was especially during the mid-to-late 19th century, in Victorian England, that macramé ruled! It was the perfect complementary craft for the already excessively ornamented and over-decorated interiors of the day.

In Turin, Italy, at the turn of the century, Cavandoli macramé was evolving. Named for the school teacher who taught it to her charges, this particular form of knotting conceals and reveals color using horizontal and vertical half hitching to create a design or picture. (See Purple Heart Pin, page 104, for an example of this creative technique.) By the 1920s, macramé had entered its dormant phase.

This article from a 1911 *Ladies Home Journal* indicates that macramé was still riding the crest of its popularity in the years just following the Victorian Age.

## Knotting's just another word for nothing else to do...

Along came the 1960s and guess what—Macramé Lives Again! Who would've guessed that the hippie-dippy Dead Heads of the '60s would have so much in common with Victorian ladies of leisure? Macramé was at the forefront of the arts and crafts renaissance of the late '60s and early '70s. It was a strange time… Nixon was president, and an entire generation was yearning for creative self-expression (as well as peace). Youthful energy flowed into batik, tie-dye, weaving, candle and jewelry making, wood crafts, leather and, oh yes, macramé. Perhaps you're old enough to remember droopy little spider plants (withered from too much incense and patchouli) in gigantic three-tiered macramé plant hangers. And what about those spooky-looking knotted owls with big wooden-bead eyes?

Big-and-awkward seemed to be the fashion trend for the early 1970s. From Elton John's gigantic glasses to alpine platform shoes…it was wide bells, wide ties, wide lapels and wide sideburns. You were stylin' if you were wearing a shag haircut, mood ring, three-prong macramé belt, hip-hugger elephant bells, tube-top, and earth shoes—reclining in your bean bag chair, listening to a Peter Frampton 8-track, and watching Mod Squad on your console television, while your mom raked the knee-high orange shag carpeting. Well, maybe that was just me.

Although the knots haven't changed a bit, *The New Macramé* bears little resemblance to the Harvest Gold and Avocado Age of knotting in the late '60s and early '70s. Today's knotting (sometimes referred to as *micro-macramé*) has an understated elegance and sophistication that reflects a more grown-up and decidedly less-is-more artistic attitude. The use of more delicate fibers, more natural and less showy embellishments, and colors that do not blind—brings a mature sense of gracefulness to contemporary knotted jewelry and accessories.

Groovy macramé vests like this were *de rigueur* during the '60s and '70s. (Dig those crazy sideburns.) PHOTO BY BERNI GORSKI, COURTESY OF DONA Z. MEILACH, *MACRAMÉ ACCESSORIES*, 1972

The new macramé is made from anything that can be tied and knotted. These earrings are made from copper wire.

# BEFORE YOU BEGIN

*One of the wonderful things about macramé is that it requires no fancy tools or expensive materials. It also requires very little space, so you can do it just about anywhere. Keep in mind that macramé is a repetitive activity and you'll be working with some rather tiny beads and delicate cords, so it's extremely important to have adequate light and to be comfortable.*

## things you need to get started

### CORD

First, you need some kind of cord to knot with. Most of the projects in this book are made with waxed linen, hemp, embroidery floss, and rattail cord. These fibers are reasonably priced, attractive, easy to knot, and are readily available at craft and jewelry supply stores. They may also be purchased from the suppliers listed in the back of the book. For practice knotting, plain old string, or seine twine will work. If you've never knotted, a thicker cord, (such as clothesline) might make learning the knots a little easier. Using several different colors of cord can also help clarify knot construction.

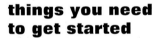

### RATTAIL

Rattail is a satiny rayon cord that's available in a variety of colors. It comes in 2.0mm (Standard #1) and 3.0mm (Heavy #2) diameter, as well 1.5mm (#0 Petite). It can be purchased by the spool or by the yard. It knots easily and the knots show up very well. It is somewhat *slippery*, which is great if you make a mistake and have to undo some of your knotting. However, it also means that your knots tend to open, so it's best to knot tightly. (When double half hitching with rattail, remember that it's just not humanly possible to make perfectly even rows.)

### SOUTACHE

A flat, ribbed rattail, soutache is commonly used as trim. Because of its shape, it's a bit less forgiving than the round rattail, but the results are particularly attractive.

### WAXED LINEN

This is an extremely popular cord for macramé jewelry. It is a bit stiff and makes well-defined, crisp knots. It is available in lots of colors and is quite agreeable to most beads. It comes in 2, 3, 4, and 7 ply. It is sold by the spool and in smaller packs. Waxed linen may tend to unravel a bit, but just give it a clockwise twist to correct. Do not get this cord soaked—don't wear it swimming, or launder it.

### HEMP

This strong, natural fiber knots and wears well. Jewelry is usually knotted with 1mm or 2mm diameter cord. *Beading* hemp twine is soft, while the *polished* is sleeker.

### POLYPROPYLENE

This was the cord of choice in the 1960s and '70s. It's strong, extremely durable and makes a darn fine plant hanger. It's available in 2, 4, 6, and 8mm. The dog collar & leash and blue shoulder bag projects use this cord.

### EMBROIDERY FLOSS

This cotton cord is available in a rainbow of colors and is sold by the skein (8.7 yards, 8 m). A word of caution—knots are very difficult to untie.

### COTTON CROCHET AND CARPET WARP THREAD

For small delicate work, these cords are great. They are soft, very easy to work with and available in lots of colors. These cords are not recommended for the novice knotter, since the density of the knotting makes it difficult to correct mistakes.

### WIRE

Wire can be a great deal of fun to knot. Check out the Heart Stopper Copper Ring and Take Two Earrings and Call me in the Morning projects. There are many different kinds of wire, but soft 24-gauge copper, or coated copper wire is best for knotting. If you already have experience working with wire, try using fine silver (sterling isn't soft enough to be practical). Wire becomes more brittle the more it is worked, so try not to 'rework' your knotting. Wire knotting is inherently looser and less even than knotting with fiber, so if you're a perfectionist, you might not enjoy this medium.

## MACRAMÉ WORK SURFACE

You can buy macramé boards, but it's just as easy to make your own. Any lightweight, portable, porous surface you can push pins into, but not through, will work. Try a ceiling tile covered with felt or paper; a block of dense foam rubber, a clipboard covered with a piece of corkboard, foam core, pieces of corrugated cardboard taped together, or polystyrene, etc. Look around your house and you'll probably find all that you need to fashion something quite suitable. NOTE: It's very important that you're comfortable when you're knotting, so try a few different things, until you find what works best for you!

## PINS

Pins are used to secure your work to the surface of your choice. T-pins are generally the easiest to use (the horizontal part of the "T" makes it easy on the fingers), and they are available in a variety of sizes. Smaller straight pins or ball pins can be used when working with more delicate cotton threads, such as embroidery floss. Pins are used most effectively when the head is slanted away from you.

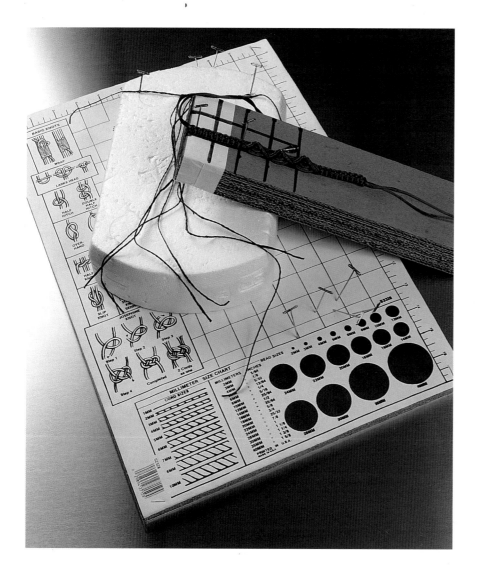

## RUBBER BANDS

Small rubber bands are very handy for securing long cords. See the section on butterfly bobbins on page 14. NOTE: For the dyslexic among us, it can be tremendously helpful to wrap your cords with different colored rubber bands. This provides an instantly recognizable key to your cords. (It's a right brain/left brain thing.)

## EMBELLISHMENTS

Whether used as finishing touches or to create colorful patterns, embellishments such as beads, baubles, bells, and charms can dramatically enhance your knotting. You'll want to make sure that the color, weight, size, and texture of the bead or bauble complements your cord. (A heavy stone bead might be beautiful, but it could overwhelm a delicate pattern and fine cord.) If you plan to knot beads directly into your project, remember that the hole in your bead must accommodate your cord(s).

You'll also need scissors, a tape measure, and clear-drying glue.

## things you should know

### A BIT MORE ABOUT BEADS

*In case of a tight fit, here are a few helpful hints:*

■ If using waxed cord, scraping a bit off the end can sometimes make stringing easier.

■ If you're met with resistance when using rattail, try dipping the ends in clear nail polish or melted wax. (Of course, allow time to dry, or you'll have a real mess on your hands.)

■ If you're obsessed with using a particular bead, you can try enlarging the hole with a file or drill.

■ A small crochet hook (#0) can be used to pull cords through beads. A tapestry needle may also be used to make stringing easier.

■ If you plan to use butterfly bobbins (see page 14), make sure to put the beads on your cords *before* you wind them up.

■ You can always sew embellishments onto your piece after you're done. And you can dangle beads by attaching them with head pins. Several of the choker projects have dangling beads that are attached in just this way.

### ATTACHING BEADS WITH HEAD PINS

**1.** Insert the head pin up through the bead or beads.

**2.** Trim the excess wire, being sure to leave about ½-inch (13mm) or slightly less. See figure 1.

**3.** Using round-nose pliers, sharply bend the wire toward you. See figure 2.

**4.** Grasp the tip of the pin and bend it away from you and around the cord you're using to form a smooth loop. See figure 3.

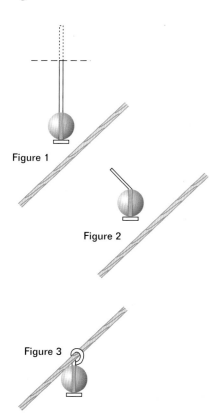

Figure 1

Figure 2

Figure 3

### JUMP RINGS

Always open and close jump rings sideways. Do not pull the ends apart. Be certain your rings are closed tightly, so your cords cannot slip out.

## EARRINGS

It's a good idea to make a pair of earrings at the same time, side-by-side on your work board. This gives you a chance to compare and contrast, as you work, and will help you keep them uniform in size and shape.

## THE LONG AND SHORT OF IT

When making one of the projects in this book, check the *finished length* and determine if that's the size you want to make. A *standard* size bracelet is approximately 7 inches (17.5 cm) long, while a *standard* size anklet is about 9 inches (22.5 cm) long. Generally, chokers are 16 inches (40 cm) long, and necklaces vary from 18 inches (45 cm) up to 35 inches (87.5 cm). But personal measurements differ as much as individual tastes. To get the results you want, you may add or subtract a few groups of knots or make your sennits a little longer or shorter.

All the projects in this book provide the necessary lengths of cords, but when you're ready to design your own knotted jewelry, how do you figure out the quantity of cord needed? Unfortunately, there isn't a scientific formula for determining exactly how long your cords should be, but the official macramé mantra is *"cut eight times the finished length."* Therefore, if you wanted to make a 7-inch (17.5 cm) bracelet, you would cut your cords 56 inches (140 cm). This assumes you will be folding your cords in half before starting your knotting. If you are not, cut your cords five times the finished length.

Knotting consumes heavier cords faster than thinner cords. (If you decide to make a project using a different weight cord, keep this in mind.)

When making sennits, the length of the anchor cords—the cords around which you knot—will not be changed at all. However, the knotting cords—the cords with which you tie the knots, will require five or six times the length of the sennit.

One thing is certain: it's much easier to trim a cord that's too long, than run short and have to add additional cord.

## ADDING CORDS

If you should run short, fear knot! You can add cord in several ways. If you are double half hitching (see figure 4) and your knot-bearer runs low, add a new cord and just knot over the two cords for a bit until your short cord runs out. In addition, if you're square knotting, you can add anchor cord without too much distress (see figure 5). If you run out of knotting cord, temporarily switch your knotting and anchor cords, add the new cord, then switch back.

Figure 4

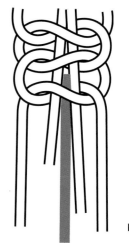

Figure 5

Of course, you're most likely to run short at a most conspicuous place. If this should happen to you, take a deep breath and just add whatever cord you need. Keep the ends of the old short cord and the new cord pinned out of your way, and press on. When you're finished with the piece, revisit the scene of the accident and carefully thread the ends to the backside of the piece and tie them off. Remember, there's no such thing as perfection and cord is cheap, so next time cut more than you think you'll need!

## BUTTERFLY BOBBINS

If you find yourself all tangled up in your cords, it's time to make your macramé life more manageable with butterfly bobbins. This is a very efficient way to keep excessive cord under control. See figure 6.

Starting about 1 foot (30 cm) from the mounting, place the cord between your thumb and index finger. Bring cord around your thumb, as shown, and wrap in a figure-eight pattern until you reach the end of the cord. Put a small rubber band around the center of the figure eight to secure; the cord can now be used without having to remove the rubber band.

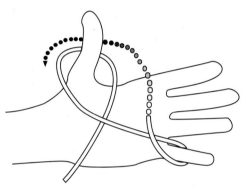

Figure 6

# KNOTS 101

It's amazing, but true…most macramé is made with just four knots: the square knot, the double half hitch, the overhand knot, and the Lark's head. What's even more amazing is the dizzying array of knot-tying variations and combinations that are available with these few knots. It is this endless variety of design possibilities that keeps macramé so fresh and makes it so much fun. None of these knots are particularly difficult to make (a little child can make a double half hitch), but it takes a bit of practice to create beautifully even and uniform rows. Making sennits and practice squares will give you the basic training you need for the great projects that are just ahead. Allow yourself the time it takes to get acquainted and comfortable with the basics, and macramé will become a rewarding activity that you'll enjoy for years to come.

Before we get into a description of the different knots, let's review some basic terms that you'll want to remember. These are also included in the glossary in the back of the book.

**ANCHOR CORD:** (A.K.A. filler and core) The cord(s) around which knots are tied. This term is most often used when referring to square knotting.

**FLOATING CORDS:** Cords that are unknotted and hang loose.

**KNOT-BEARER:** (A.K.A. leader cord) The cord(s) around which knots are tied. This term is most often used when referring to double half hitching.

**KNOTTING CORD:** The cord(s) with which knots are tied.

**ROW:** A series of knots made next to each other in a straight line.

**SENNIT:** A length of continuously knotted cord.

# LARK'S HEAD KNOT

*(A.K.A. Mounting Knot, Reverse Double Half Hitch, and Cow Hitch)* Macramé pieces are traditionally begun with this knot. Knotting cords are mounted or attached to a taut stationary cord (holding cord), jump ring, buckle, etc., with this knot.

Fold a knotting cord in half. Pass the looped end of the knotting cord behind the holding cord, from the top down. Bring the loose ends of the knotting cord over the holding cord and through the loop. Tighten.

## REVERSE LARK'S HEAD KNOT

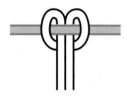

Pass the looped end of the knotting cord behind the holding cord, from the bottom up. Fold the loop over the holding cord and bring the loose ends through. Pull to tighten.

## VERTICAL LARK'S HEAD KNOT

A knotting cord (or cords) is looped twice around a vertical anchor cord (or cords) in this variation.

Bring the knotting cord over the anchor; loop it around to the top and down. The second loop goes under the anchor, around to the top, and down.

## ALTERNATING LARK'S HEAD SENNIT

This knot is worked by tying a vertical Lark's head knot around an anchor cord with the left knotting cord, then the right, then the left, etc.

## DOUBLE ALTERNATING LARK'S HEAD SENNIT

This popular knotting pattern is worked by intertwining two alternating Lark's head sennits. (The Yuppie-Puppy Collar on page 000 is an example of this pattern.) The illustration shows the pattern worked around two anchor cords. Four anchor cords are used in the photo.

# HALF KNOT

(*A.K.A. Macramé Knot*) This knot is actually the first half of the square knot. It is generally made with four cords and can be started from either the right or the left. (To help remember how to tie these knots just remember: "over, under, under, up".)

### Left-Handed Half Knot

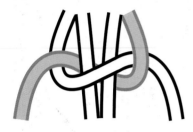

Pass the left-hand cord over the anchor cords and under the right-hand cord, leaving a little loop on the left. Pass the right-hand cord under the anchor cords and up through the loop. Gently pull the knotting cords to tighten.

### Right-Handed Half Knot

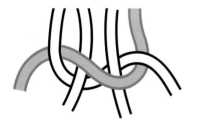

Pass the right-hand cord over the anchor cords and under the left-hand cord, leaving a little loop on the right. Pass the left-hand cord under the anchor cords and up through the loop. Gently pull the knotting cords to tighten.

## HALF KNOT SENNIT

A continuous chain of half knots will produce a twisting effect. After about four knots, the sennit will begin to twist in the opposite direction from which the knot was started. A full twist requires about eight knots. These knots should be tied very tightly.

## SQUARE KNOT

(*A.K.A. Flat Knot and Reef Knot*) The good news is you already know how to make the first half of this knot. Remember, a square knot is made up of two half knots.

Once you've tied a half knot, all you need to do is to make another half knot in the opposite direction!

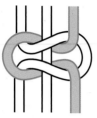 

Square knots are typically tied around two anchor cords.

But square knots can be tied around any number of anchor cords. (Multiple cords may be used as knotting cords.)

Sennits made from square knots are particularly popular and attractive.

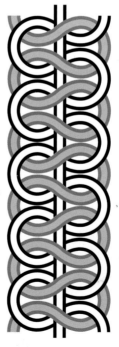 

## Left-Handed Square Knot

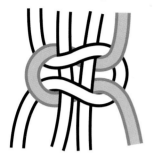

First, make a left-handed half knot. Now bring the cord on the right over the anchor cords and under the left-hand cord. Pass the left-hand cord under the anchor cords and up through the loop on the right. Gently pull the knotting cords to tighten.

## Right-Handed Square Knot

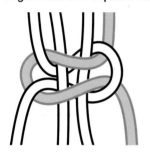

First, make a right-handed half knot. Now bring the cord on the left over the anchor cords and under the right hand cord. Pass the right-hand cord under the anchor cords and up through the loop on the left.

## Square Knots with Interchangeable Anchor and Knotting Cords

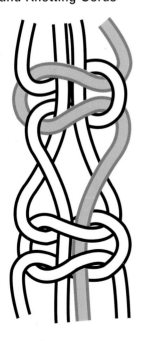

Alternating your anchor cords with your knotting cords, between square knots, creates an interesting pattern. You might also try this if your knotting cords are getting used up too fast.

## ALTERNATING SQUARE KNOTS

This very popular technique offers all sorts of interesting pattern variations. In the typical arrangement, the first row of square knots is made in the usual way. The first and last two cords of the second row are floated. The third row is knotted the same as the first. (The Blue Beauty Shoulder Bag on page 86 is a great example of this classic style.)

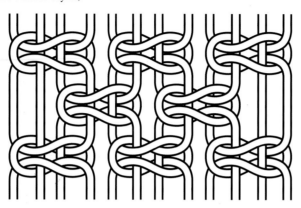

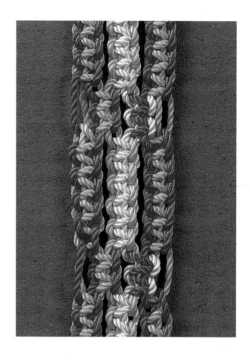

## HALF HITCH

(*A.K.A. Buttonhole Loop*) The half hitch is (big surprise) the first half of the double half hitch. It may be used in any of the ways the double half hitch is used, but it is not often used by itself, since it is just a single loop.

A single loop is made around one (or more) knot-bearing cord(s).

A sennit of half hitches will have a spiral or corkscrew appearance.

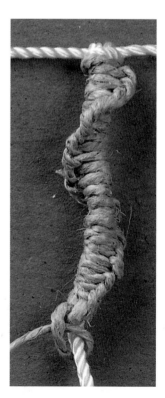

A double loop is made around one (or more) knot-bearing cord(s).

# DOUBLE HALF HITCH

(*A.K.A. Clove Hitch*) This knot shares the spotlight with the square knot in the macramé Hall of Fame. Looping a knotting cord over an anchor cord twice makes the double half hitch. It may be made from either left to right or right to left. What really gives this knot its tremendous versatility is the angle at which the knot-bearer is held.

## Horizontal Double Half Hitch

The anchor cord is held taut over the knotting cords in a horizontal direction. The knotting cords are then looped twice around the knot-bearer to form double half hitches.

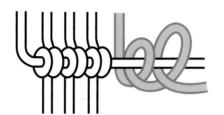

## Diagonal Double Half Hitch

The knot-bearer is held taut over the knotting cords in a diagonal direction. The knotting cords are then looped twice around the knot-bearer to form double half hitches. The popular X- and V-shaped patterns are formed in this manner.

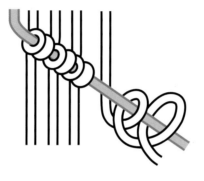

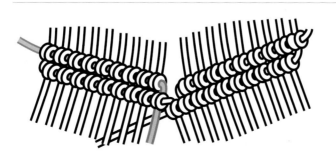

### Vertical Double Half Hitch

In this variation, the knot-bearer and knotting cords trade places. There is only a single knotting cord. The knot-bearers are held taut *under* the knotting cord in a vertical direction, and the knotting cord is looped twice around the knot-bearers to form double half hitches.

## OVERHAND KNOT

Most often used as a gathering knot, to secure beads, or to prevent the fraying at the end of a cord. This knot can be made using just one cord, a group of cords, or tied around an anchor cord.

Make a loop. Bring the end of the cord behind the loop and out through the loop. Pull tight.

### Alternating Overhand Knot

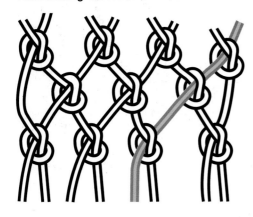

This technique is often used for bags and hammocks. It resembles netting. The left-hand cord is tied around the right-hand cord. The first and third rows are the same. The first and last cords float in the second row.

## COIL KNOT

This is very similar to the overhand knot and is generally used to finish the ends of cords.

Make a large overhand knot, but before you pull it tight, wrap the end around the loop five or six more times. Pull ends to tighten and the *coil* appears as if by macramé magic!

## JOSEPHINE KNOT

(*A.K.A. Carrick Bend and Chinese Knot*) This is an oval-shaped knot, made by intertwining two loops (of one or more cords). It is especially decorative when made with multiple cords. Keep your cords flat and parallel, and try using two different colors for greater definition. This knot is often made loosely and may be made in either direction. After you master making it as shown, try reversing the direction. If this doesn't send you directly to dyslexia hell, press on!

Make a loop in a counterclockwise direction with the left-hand cord, so the loop faces to the right. Bring the right-hand cord over the loop and weave it under the lower end of the loop, over the upper end, under the top of the loop, over itself and finally under the bottom of the loop.

## BELIEVE IT OR "KNOT"...

With experience, you'll be able to look at a piece of macramé and actually read the knots. Once you reach the point of being able to recognize knots in this way you may refer to yourself as: *Macramé Maestro*, *Macramé Mistress*, *Macramé Master*, or just plain old *Knot-Head*.

# MACRAMÉ GALLERY

Just in case you need a bit of knotting inspiration, here are some unique and beautiful pieces to whet your creative appetite. Look at the incredible artistic diversity of these works and remember that they're all made using the same few knots. That's what makes macramé so magical.

**NECKLACES BY JANE OLSON**

ABOVE: **PINK COTTON SHELL PENDANT NECKLACE WITH SMALL BEADS**

LEFT AND DETAIL: **GRAY LINEN NECKLACE WITH CARVED CHINESE STONES**

PHOTOS BY THE ARTIST

FAR LEFT: **BEADED NECKLACES.**
Lynn Smythe

LEFT: **EYEGLASS CASE.**
Jim Gentry

BELOW: **NAUTICAL KNOTTED
NECKLACES.** Elaine Lieberman

PHOTOS BY EVAN BRACKEN

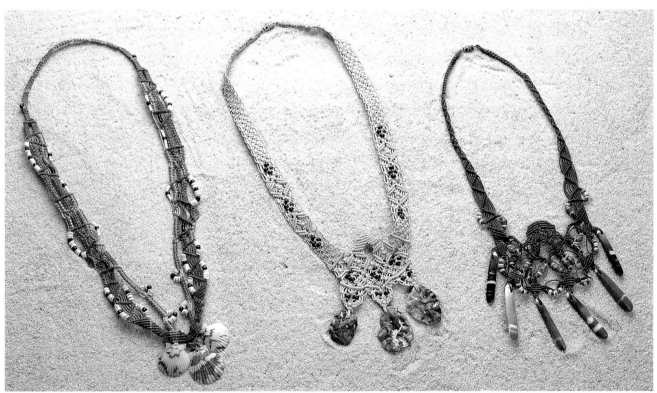

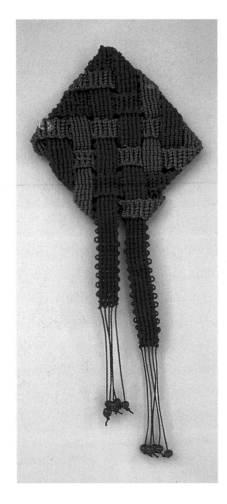

JEWELRY BY ROXY MOSTELLER

ABOVE: **RED WOVEN PENDANT**

RIGHT: **BEAR'S PAW PENDANT NECKLACE AND EARRINGS**

PHOTOS BY STEVEN ROOS

JEWELRY BY SANDY SWIRNOFF

TOP LEFT AND DETAIL BELOW: *CIRCLES IN TIME I.* NYLON CORD, K. OVINGTON GLASS DISCS, AND SEED BEADS. PHOTOS BY MELINDA HOLDEN

TOP RIGHT AND DETAIL BELOW: *MACRAMÉ LACE.* SILVER LEAF AGATE, PEARLS, SEED BEADS, AND SILVER. PHOTOS BY NEL YTSMA

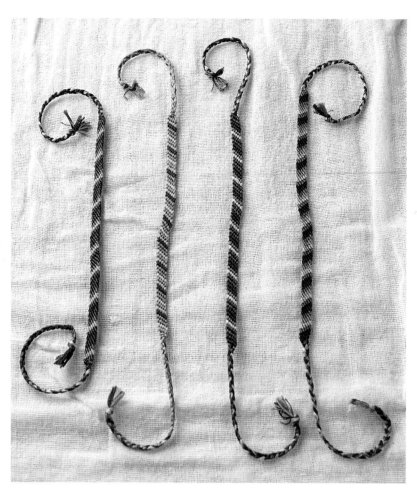

RIGHT: **FRIENDSHIP BRACELETS. Jim Gentry**
BOTTOM RIGHT: **A GREEN JADE NECKLACE. Sandy Swirnoff**
BELOW: **WAXED TAN CIRCLE. Elaine Lieberman**

PHOTOS BY EVAN BRACKEN

SCULPTURE BY JOH RICCI

TOP LEFT: *WHIRLWIND.* NYLON, BRASS HEISHI, SEED BEADS, QUARTZ

BOTTOM LEFT: *SOUTHWEST HORIZON.* NYLON, HAKE GLASS

TOP AND BOTTOM RIGHT: *FOUR SEASON PEPPER.* NYLON AND SEED BEADS

PHOTOS BY THE ARTIST

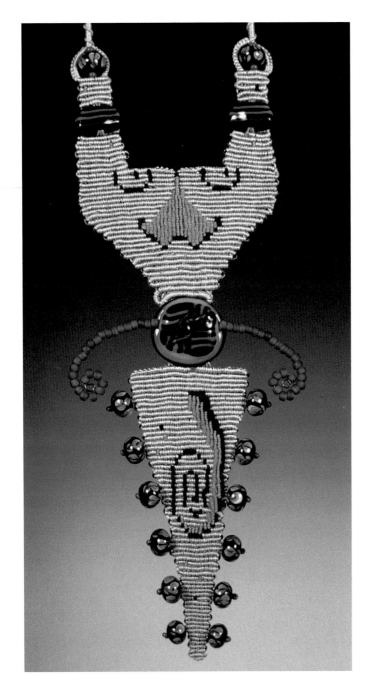

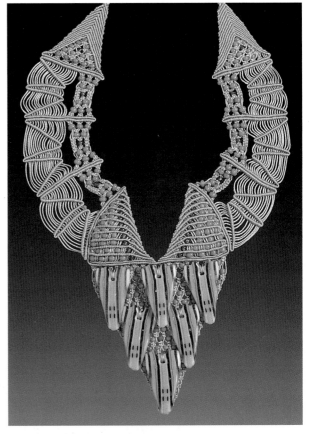

JEWELRY BY BERNADETTE MAHFOOD

ABOVE: *MORNING GLORY SMILE.* NECKPIECE WITH GLASS BEADS

TOP RIGHT: *AFRICA REVISITED.* ANTIQUE BEADS, FLAME-WORKED
GLASS BEADS

BOTTOM RIGHT: BIB AND COLLAR WITH FORMED GLASS PIECES
AND SEED BEADS

PHOTOS BY LARRY SANDERS

TOP LEFT: **FINE SILVER EARRINGS.** Elaine Lieberman

TOP RIGHT: **BLUE WITH PEACOCK PEARLS.** Elaine Lieberman

LEFT: **ASSORTED WIRE NECKLACES.** Elaine Lieberman

PHOTOS BY EVAN BRACKEN

ACCESSORIES AND JEWELRY
BY DR. KEITH RUSSELL

CLOCKWISE FROM RIGHT:

**PURSE**

**EARRINGS**

**EARRINGS**

**NECK PIECE**

**WOOL BELT**

PHOTOS BY TERENCE HOLLOW

ABOVE: **ASSORTED BOOKMARKS.**
(LEFT TO RIGHT) **Jim Gentry, Elaine Lieberman,**
(REMAINING THREE) **Pat Thibodeaux**

LEFT: **HEMP NECKLACE WITH CORAL BEADS.**
**Jim Gentry**

PHOTOS BY EVAN BRACKEN

# WONDERFUL Y NECKLACE

*This wonderful necklace features soft-to-the-skin dyed hemp, accent e-beads,
an attractive alternating anchor/knotting cord pattern and classic Y design.*

DESIGNER: **ELAINE LIEBERMAN**

## FINISHED LENGTH

Approximately 16 inches (70 cm) around the neck, 2½-inch (6.3 cm) center drop. (To make a longer necklace, cut your cords 1 foot [30 cm] longer per 3½ inches [8.8 cm] of additional desired length.)

## KNOTS USED

Square knot, half knot, overhand

## MATERIALS

Thin dyed hemp
• 4 cords cut 4½ feet (135 cm) each
17 e-beads, to match or contrast
2 jump rings (6mm)
1 barrel clasp

## TOOLS

Measuring tape
Scissors
Macramé work board
T-pins
Clear-drying glue
Chain-nose pliers

*This necklace is started at the bottom or base of the Y. The attractive pattern is created by making two square knots, switching your anchor and knotting cords, making two square knots, and switching, etc. Be consistent with the space used to switch cords.*

## INSTRUCTIONS

**1.** String seven beads onto one of your cords and position them at the center point of the cord. This cord will be your anchor cord. Let's call it cord A.

**2.** Fold another cord in half and position under cord A. These will be your knotting cords. Let's refer to this as cord B. The fold point of cord B should be just beneath the loop of beads.

**3.** Make two square knots with cord B around cord A. (Secure your work to the knotting board with T-pins.)

**4.** Switch your anchor cords with the knotting cords. Leave about ¼ inch (6mm) between the bottom of your last square knot and the top of the next.

**5.** Make two square knots.

**6.** Repeat step 4.

**7.** Repeat step 5.

**8.** Repeat step 4, again.

**9.** Make one square knot.

**10.** String a bead onto each of your knotting cords.

**11.** Make another square knot.

*Now it's time to split our necklace into the two prongs of the Y shape. We'll make the left side first, then go back and make the right side.*

**12.** Use your two left-hand cords as anchor cords, and fold a new cord in half and position it under your anchor cords (just as you did in step 2). These new cords will be your knotting cords.

**13.** Make one square knot.

**14.** String one bead onto each of your knotting cords, and tie another square knot.

**15.** Repeat step 4.

**16.** Repeat step 5.

**17.** Repeat step 4.

**18.** Repeat step 5.

**19.** Repeat step 4.

**20.** Repeat step 11.

**21.** Repeat step 12.

**22.** Continue to switch your anchor and knotting cords, each time making two square knots, until the length is around 6½ inches (16 cm).

**23.** Alternate your cords once more and make four square knots.

**24.** Firmly tie your knotting cords together, with an overhand knot, in the back of the necklace. Move these cords out of your way; you are done with them for the moment.

**25.** Fold your anchor cords around a jump ring from the front to back.

*Leave just enough room between the last square knot you made and the jump ring, to make four more square knots. You have folded your anchor cords back toward your knotting. This gives you the new knotting cords you need to make four more square knots.*

**26.** Make four more square knots.

**27.** Firmly tie your new knotting cords together, with an overhand knot, in the back of the necklace.

**28.** Trim all cords to ¼ inch (6mm).

**29.** Glue the knots and ends to the back of the necklace. Allow to dry.

**30.** Add the clasp.

**31.** Repeat steps 12–30 on the other side to complete the necklace.

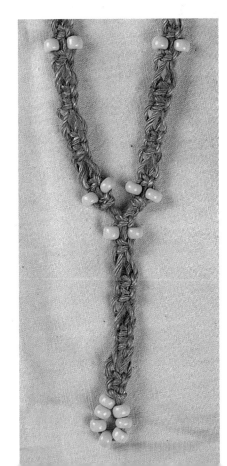

# BRACELET/ANKLET/CHOKER COMBO

*Here's a winning combination—an alternating anchor/knotting cord pattern, accent seed beads, simple square knots, and easy-to-knot waxed linen.*

DESIGNER: **ELAINE LIEBERMAN**

## Bracelet and Anklet

**FINISHED LENGTH**

Bracelet is 7 inches (17.5 cm)
Anklet is 9 inches (22.5)

**KNOTS USED**

Square, overhand

**MATERIALS**

4-ply waxed linen

- 2 cords cut 4 feet (120 cm) each (Bracelet)
- 2 cords cut 5 feet (150 cm) each (Anklet)

18 size 8 seed beads (Bracelet)

26 size 8 seed beads (Anklet)

1 jump or split ring 6–9mm (Bracelet)

1 jump or split ring 6–9mm (Anklet)

1 jump ring 4–5mm (Bracelet)

1 jump ring 4–5 mm (Anklet)

1 self-closing clasp (Bracelet)

1 self-closing clasp (Anklet)

**TOOLS**

Measuring tape

Scissors

Macramé work board

T-pins

Chain-nose pliers

Clear-drying glue

**INSTRUCTIONS**

**1.** Fold and center your two cords through the larger jump or split ring. You will now have four cords of equal length. Secure your work to the knotting board with a T-pin through the jump ring.

**2.** Make eight square knots.

**3.** Switch your anchor cords with the knotting cords. Leave about 3/16-inch (5mm) between the bottom of your last square knot and the top of the next.

**4.** Make one square knot.

**5.** String one bead onto each of your knotting cords.

**6.** Make one more square knot.

**7.** Repeat step 3–6.

**8.** Continue this pattern until you have made nine pairs of square knots (or 13 pairs of square knots for an anklet).

**9.** Alternate your cords once more and make four square knots.

**10.** Firmly tie your knotting cords together, with an overhand knot, in the back of the bracelet (anklet). Move these cords out of your way; you are done with them for the moment.

**11.** Fold your anchor cords around a jump ring from the front to back. Leave just enough room between the last square knot you made and the jump ring to make four more square knots. You have folded your anchor cords back toward the knotting. This gives you the new knotting cords you need to make four more square knots.

**12.** Make four more square knots.

**13.** Firmly tie your new knotting cords together, with an overhand knot, in the back of the bracelet (anklet).

**14.** Trim all cords to 1/4 inch (6mm).

**15.** Glue the knots and ends to the back of the bracelet (anklet). Allow to dry.

**16.** Open the jump ring, add the clasp, and close.

# Tie Choker

## FINISHED LENGTH

Approximately 28 inches
(70 cm) end to end

## KNOTS USED

Overhand and square

## MATERIALS

7-ply waxed linen
- 2 cords cut 5 feet
  (150 cm) each
- 1 cord cut 2 yards (1.8 m)

26 e-beads

## TOOLS

Measuring tape
Scissors
Macramé work board
T-pins
Clear-drying glue

## INSTRUCTIONS

**1.** Tie your two 5-foot (150 cm) cords together with an overhand knot approximately 1 foot (30 cm) from the ends. These will be your anchor cords. Secure to your knotting board with a T-pin through the knot.

**2.** Fold your other cord in half and place it beneath the cords you just tied. The center point should be just below the overhand knot. These will be your knotting cords.

**3.** Make five square knots.

**4.** Switch your anchor cords with your knotting cords. Leave about ¼ inch (6mm) between the bottom of your last square knot and the top of the next.

**5.** Make one square knot.

**6.** String a bead onto each of your knotting cords.

**7.** Make another square knot.

**8.** Repeat steps 4–7.

**9.** Continue this pattern until the knotted part of your choker is approximately 9 inches (22.5 cm) long. The last knotting cords you use should be the longer ones…this means you will have an odd number of square knots with paired beads.

**10.** Switch your anchor cords with the knotting cords. The longer cords are now your anchors.

**11.** Make five square knots.

**12.** Make an overhand knot using just your anchor cords. Tie this close to the last square knot.

**13.** Firmly tie your knotting cords together, with an overhand knot, in the back of the choker.

**14.** Cut your knotting cords, leaving around ¼ inch (6mm).

**15.** Glue the knot and end to the back of the choker. Let dry.

**16.** Cut the anchor cords on either end approximately 10 inches (25 cm) from each overhand knot.

**17.** Tie overhand knots on either end, using anchor cords, about ½ inch (13mm) from each end.

**18.** Glue the knots and ends of the cords. Let dry.

# TIME IN A BOTTLE WATCH

*Update your favorite wristwatch with a nifty new knotted band. Here's a handsome blend of square knots, double half hitch crosses, subtle accent beads, and a dazzling shank button clasp. It all adds up to truly timely fashion!*

DESIGNER: **LYNN SMYTHE**

**FINISHED LENGTH**

To fit your wrist

**KNOTS USED**

Lark's head, square, double half hitch

**MATERIALS**

4-ply brown waxed linen
- 4 cords cut 30 inches (75 cm) each
- 4 cords cut 40 inches (100 cm) each

Watch face

32 round copper beads (2mm)

1 shank button, for clasp

**TOOLS**

Measuring tape

Scissors

Macramé work board

T-pins, or heavy straight pins

Clear nail polish

Blunt end tapestry needle

Locking hemostats or pliers

**INSTRUCTIONS**

**1.** Fold the four 30-inch (75 cm) cords in half, and mount with Lark's head knots to the top pin of the watch face.

**2.** Secure to your work board using T-pins through the bottom pin of the watch face.

**3.** Number your cords 1–8, from left to right.

**4.** Tie one square knot with cords 1–4 and one square knot with cords 5–8.

**5.** Make a square knot with cords 3–6.

**6.** String one 2mm copper bead on cord 1 and one bead on cord 8.

**7.** Repeat step 4.

**8.** Repeat step 5.

**9.** Repeat step 6.

**10.** Repeat step 4.

**11.** Repeat step 5.

**12.** String one 2mm copper bead on cord 4 and one bead on cord 5.

**13.** Form an X-shape with diagonal double half hitches, as shown. First, use cord 1 as the knot-bearer and make the double half hitches with cords 2, 3, and 4. Then, use cord 8 as the knot-bearer and knot with cords 7–2. Finish the X pattern by double half hitching cords 5, 6, and 7 around 1. (Remember to keep your knot-bearers taut as you work.)

**14.** Repeat step 12.

**15.** Repeat step 5.

**16.** Repeat steps 4, 5, and 6.

**17.** Repeat steps 4, 5, and 6, again.

**18.** Repeat step 4.

**19.** Now, make four square knots, but this time cords 3, 4, 5, and 6 will be used as our anchor cords. Use cords 1 and 2 as your left knotting cords, and 7 and 8 as your right knotting cords.

**20.** Remove your pins from the knotting board. Flip your watch over, and secure again.

**21.** String your shank button onto cords 4 and 5. (The button should face down.)

**22.** Using cords 4 and 5 as your anchor cords, tie one square knot around the button. Cords 1, 2, and 3 are your left knotting cords, and cords 6, 7, and 8 are your right knotting cords.

**23.** String one 2 mm copper bead on the end of cord 1, followed by an overhand knot.

**24.** Use a T-pin to move the knot as close to the bead as possible. Then, trim the cord close to the knot.

**25.** Brush a drop of clear nail polish on the knot and let dry completely.

**26.** Finish off cords 2–8 in the same manner.

**27.** Now let's make the bottom portion of the watchband. Use the remaining four 40-inch (100 cm) cords and repeat steps 1–19.

**28.** Move cords 1 and 2 and cords 7 and 8 out of your way. (Wrap them around T-pins secured to your working board, if you like.)

**29.** Now, tie approximately 23 square knots. Cords 4 and 5 are your anchor cords, and cords 3 and 6 are your knotting cords.

**NOTE:** *This last length of square knots is approximate, so that you can make the band a little shorter or a little longer, to fit your wrist.*

**30.** Fold this last section of square knots back on itself, making a loop large enough to snugly fit the button clasp.

**31.** Temporarily secure this loop in place with the hemostats or pliers. Try on the watchband, and add or subtract square knots to get an exact fit.

**32.** Once you get a perfect fit, secure the loop onto the strap by tying 4 to 6 square knots. You are still using cords 3 and 6 as your knotters. Cords 4 and 5 (*plus the watchband*) are your anchors. Cords 1 and 2, and 7 and 8 are still moved out of the way.

**33.** Use the tapestry needle to bury each cord end into the watchband. You can use the hemostats or pliers to assist you in pulling the needle.

**34.** Cut each cord as close to the knotting as possible. Secure each cut end with a little dab of clear nail polish and let dry.

# BRUSHED HEMP TASSEL PULL

*This decorative pull has a half knot twist handle and soft fluffy tassel. It's a breeze to make and adds a wonderful splash of color. Hang it from a light, a ceiling fan, or make a pair to use as curtain tiebacks.*

DESIGNER: **MARISANDE FISHER**

**FINISHED LENGTH**

Approximately 15 inches (37.5 cm)

**KNOTS USED**

Overhand, half, square

**MATERIALS**

FOR THE TASSEL

50 yards (45 m) of thin unwaxed hemp twine

- 150 cords cut 1 foot (30 cm) each
- 2 cords cut 6 inches (15 cm) each

FOR THE HANDLE

13 yards (11.5 m) 1mm braided hemp

- 1 cord cut 8 feet (2.4 m)
- 1 cord cut 8 yards (7.2 m)

**TOOLS**

Measuring tape

Scissors

Macramé work board

T-pins

Fine-toothed metal comb (a small flea comb works great!)

## INSTRUCTIONS

### to make the handle

**1.** Fold your 8-foot long (2.3 m) cord in fourths.

**2.** Tie an overhand knot in the end that has the loose ends. (The other end has two loops.) These will be the anchor cords for your handle.

**3.** Secure to your knotting board with a pin through the overhand knot.

**4.** Fold the 8-yard (7.2 m) cord in half, and place the center point under the anchor cords about an inch from the overhand knot. (Wrap your long cords into butterfly bobbins, if desired. See page 14.)

**5.** Begin tying half knots. The cords will begin to twist, naturally. Keep your knotting very tight.

**6.** Cover the length of your anchor cords with continuous half knots. Stop when you're about 2 inches (5 cm) from the end.

**7.** Bring the ends together. This will be the base of your handle. Wrap your knotting cords around the other ends, and make several firm square knots to secure. A small bulge at this joining point is fine. Trim the ends to about ¼-inch (6mm). This completes the handle.

### to make the tassel

**8.** On a smooth, flat surface, arrange the 1-foot (30 cm) cords in a flat horizontal bundle. Make sure the ends are even.

**9.** Place the handle base on the bundle, just slightly off center, as shown below.

**10.** Slide the 6-inch (15 cm) piece of hemp twine under the bundle, to the center point. Bring the ends together and tie a loose half knot. Gradually tighten the knot while keeping the twine pieces arranged evenly around the handle base. When the knot is very tight and the center feels secure, tie another tight half knot.

**11.** Pick up the handle and smooth down the ends of the tassel.

### to wrap the tassel

**12.** Use the remaining cord to wrap the tassel. Place one end of the wrapping cord over the area to be wrapped (have the end facing the bottom). Wrap a few times to secure the end.

**13.** Fold another 6-inch (15 cm) piece of scrap twine in half, and lay it over this wrapped area. (The loop should face the bottom.)

**14.** Continue wrapping from the top to the bottom, for at least ½-inch (13mm).

**15.** Thread the end of your wrapping cord through the loop. Pull on the ends of the scrap twine to draw the wrapping cord up. This will make your wrapping secure and conceal the end.

**16.** Pull the end all the way through and trim the end closely.

**17.** To create a big fluffy tassel—carefully brush out the ends with the flea comb. This takes a bit of time and patience, but creates a wonderful look!

*Here's a beautiful combination of basic knotting, exquisite color and shapes, and elegant design. This necklace has a primitive feel that's both soothing and sensual.*

DESIGNER: **PAT THIBODEAUX**

**FINISHED LENGTH**

Approximately 16 inches (40 cm) long

**KNOTS USED**

Lark's head, overhand, Josephine, square

**MATERIALS**

4-ply waxed linen
- 8 cords cut 5 feet (150 cm) each
- 2 cords cut 5 inches (12.5 cm) each

1 donut bead (25mm Carnelian pictured)

12 metal tube beads

2 faceted metal beads

12 carnelian-colored horn beads

8 small round metal beads (optional)

1 metal (flying saucer shaped) bead for clasp

**TOOLS**

Measuring tape

Scissors

Macramé work board

T-pins

**INSTRUCTIONS**

**1.** Fold your eight cords in half to find their centers, and mount them to the large donut bead with one Lark's head knot.

**2.** Tie an overhand knot just below the Lark's head knot. Secure your work to the knotting board.

**3.** You now have 16 working cords. Divide these into two groups of eight.

*We'll make the left side of this necklace first, then the right.*

**4.** Using the eight cords on your left side, divide into two groups of four cords each. Tie a Josephine knot with the two groups.

**5.** Leave about a ¼-inch (6mm) space and gather all eight cords. Tie an overhand knot.

**6.** Number your cords from left to right, 1–8.

**7.** On cords 3, 4, 5, and 6, string one horn bead, followed by one metal tube and another horn bead.

**8.** Tie a loose square knot under the beads using cords 1, 2, 7, and 8 as your knotting cords.

**9.** Spread your knotting cords out to make picots, and tighten your square knot.

**10.** On cords 3, 4, 5, and 6, string one faceted metal bead.

**11.** Repeat steps 8 and 9.

**12.** Repeat step 7.

**13.** Tie an overhand knot with all your cords. Leave about a ¼-inch (6mm) space.

**14.** Tie a Josephine knot and leave about a ¼-inch (6mm) space.

**15.** Tie an overhand knot.

**16.** Use your longest four cords as knotting cords, and tie 10 half knots. (This will make a twist.)

**17.** Tie an overhand knot. All the cords should be about the same length now. If necessary, trim up the ends to make them even.

**18.** Take four cords and twist them tightly together in a clockwise direction. Tape the end, or hold firmly. Repeat with the other four cords.

**19.** Tie an overhand knot with all eight cords about 1½ inches (3.8 cm) from the ends. String the metal (flying saucer) bead onto the cords, and tie another overhand knot.

**20.** These two cords will begin to twist together counterclockwise, naturally. Twist them together tightly, by hand, to form a "rope."

**21.** This completes side one of the necklace. Move to the other side and repeat steps 4 through 20. In step 19, omit the metal bead and finish with just the overhand knots. To tie the necklace, make an opening for the metal bead by separating the two twisted cords between the overhand knots.

**22.** To finish, mount the remaining two cords with Lark's head knots onto the outside cords, between the first overhand and Josephine knots.

**23.** String with remaining beads, as shown and secure with overhand knots. Trim ends.

# CONVERTIBLE EYEGLASSES LEASH

*Here's an eye-catching idea! A rattail strap-for-your-specs with square knots and diagonal double half hitches that cleverly converts to a fun necklace.*

DESIGNER: **ELAINE LIEBERMAN**

## FINISHED LENGTH

Approximately 13 inches (32.5 cm)

## KNOTS USED

Square, diagonal double half hitch, overhand

## MATERIALS

#1 (2mm) rattail
- 4 cords cut 8 feet (2.4 m) each

4 jump rings (9mm)

15 glass crow beads

2 self-closing clasps

1 pair eyeglass findings

## TOOLS

Measuring tape

Scissors

Macramé work board

T-pins

Chain-nose pliers

Clear-drying glue

**NOTE:** *We'll make this leash/necklace in three stages. First, we'll make the left side. Then, we'll make the right side. Finally we'll join forces, for the grand finale! It's a snap!*

## INSTRUCTIONS

**1.** String two cords of rattail through a jump ring to the center points. Secure your work to the knotting board, using a T-pin. You now have four working cords that are 4 feet (120 cm) each, centered on a jump ring.

**2.** Make four square knots.

**3.** String one bead onto your anchor or filler cords.

**4.** Make four more square knots.

**5.** Make two rows of diagonal double half hitches, working from right to left. The cord furthest right is your knot-bearing cord. Use a T-pin to keep your knot-bearer taut.

**6.** Repeat step 2.

**7.** Repeat step 3.

**8.** Repeat step 4

**9.** Make two rows of diagonal double half hitches, this time from left to right. The cord furthest left is your knot-bearing cord. Use a T-pin to keep your knot-bearer taut.

**10.** Repeat step 2, again.

**11.** Repeat step 3, again.

**12.** Repeat step 4, again.

**13.** Repeat step 5.

**14.** Repeat step 2, once more with feeling.

**15.** Repeat step 3, once more with feeling.

**16.** Repeat step 9.

**17.** Make four more square knots.

*Okay, now stop! Let's put this aside for a minute and make the other part of our eyeglass leash. We need another jump ring and our other two rattail cords. Second verse same as the first…except this time whenever you make the rows of diagonal double half hitches, make them in the opposite direction than you did before. So, follow steps 1 through 17 exactly, except in steps 5 and 13, work from left to right. In steps 9 and 16, work from right to left. When you finish this, it's time to join forces!*

**18.** Pin your work to the knotting board so the first piece you made is on the left and the side you just finished is on the right. Make sure both pieces are even and lined up.

**19.** Number your cords, from left to right, 1 through 8.

**20.** Join the left and right sides with a square knot using cords 3–6.

**21.** Make a square knot using cords 1–4.

**22.** Make another square knot using cords 5–8.

**23.** Make one more square knot using cords 3–6.

**24.** Using cord 1 as your knot-bearer, make a row of diagonal double half hitches with cords 2, 3, and 4. Work from left to right.

**25.** Using cord 8 as your knot-bearer, make a row of diagonal double half hitches with cords 7, 6, and 5. Work from right to left.

**26.** String a bead onto cords 4 and 5, (the knot-bearers that just met in the middle). Secure with an overhand knot about ¾ inch (1.9 cm) below.

**27.** Repeat step 26 with each remaining cord.

**28.** Tie a second overhand knot on top of the ones you made in step 27. (This adds extra strength and will prevent the knots from coming undone.)

**29.** Trim the cords about ½ inch (13mm) below the knots.

**30.** Attach the self-closing clasps to the jump rings at the ends of the leash.

**31.** Attach the eyeglass findings to the remaining jump rings, and finally attach these to the clasps.

# FRINGE BENEFIT BELT

*This alternating double-diamond motif sash comes with a wonderful benefits package…it's easy to make, fun to wear, stylish and versatile, comfortable, and oh so accommodating to fluctuating waistlines. So, let's get to work!*

DESIGNER: **ELAINE LIEBERMAN**

*This belt is begun in the center, and worked to one end. Then the board is turned, and it is worked to the other end. This makes it easier to work with the very long cords. When you begin work on the second side of the belt, you can reverse the direction of your square knots, if you want to be uniform. You might want to wind your active cords into butterfly bobbins to keep things manageable (see page 14). If you need to move your work around, you can keep your inactive cords in a bag taped to your board. Make yourself comfortable!*

## INSTRUCTIONS

**1.** Find the center point of each cord.

**2.** Tie all the cords together at their center points, using a very loose overhand knot.

**3.** Pin your cords through the overhand knot to your knotting board.

**4.** Number your cords 1–12, from left to right. (Remember, the numbers represent the *positions* of the cords, not the actual cords.)

*Let's make a diamond shape filled with square knots. First, we'll make the top of the diamond shape.*

**5.** Use cord 7 as your knot-bearer and make a row of diagonal double half hitches from center to left, with cords 6–1. Make sure you keep your knot-bearer taut and diagonal.

**6.** Use cord 7 (the cord that is now in the 7th position) as knot-bearer and make a row of diagonal double half hitches from center to right, using cords 8–12.

**7.** Repeat step 6.

**8.** Use cord 6 as knot-bearer and make a second row of diagonal double half hitches from center to left, with cords 5–1.

*This completes the top half of our diamond. Now, let's fill it with four square knots.*

**9.** Make a square knot with cords 5–8.

**10.** Make a square knot with cords 3–6.

**11.** Make a square knot with cords 7–10.

**12.** Repeat step 9.

*That's it for the square knots. Now, let's make the bottom part of our diamond.*

**13.** Use cord 1 as your knot-bearer and make a row of diagonal double half hitches from left to center, using cords 2–6.

**14.** Use cord 12 as your knot-bearer and make a row of diagonal double half hitches from right to center, using cords 11–7.

**15.** Repeat step 14.

**16.** Use cord 1 as your knot-bearer and make a row of diagonal double half hitches from left to right, using cords 2–12.

*This finishes our diamond shape filled with square knots and gets us started on the top part of our next diamond that will have an "X" in the center.*

## FINISHED LENGTH

To determine length, multiply your waist size by 4.5 and then add 6 feet (1.8 m). This is the length you should cut your cords.

## KNOTS USED

Overhand, double half hitch, square

## MATERIALS

12 cords of #1 rattail (cut to fit)
18 crow beads

## TOOLS

Measuring tape
Scissors
T-pins
Macramé work board
Clear-drying glue

**17.** Repeat step 8, twice.

**18.** Repeat step 6.

*That finishes the top portion of our next diamond, now we'll make the small X that goes inside the diamond shape.*

**19.** Use cord 4 as your knot-bearer and make two diagonal double half hitches, using cords 5 and 6.

**20.** Use cord 9 as your knot-bearer and make three diagonal double half hitches, using cords 8, 7, and 6.

**21.** Make two more double half hitches on each knot bearer, to finish the "X".

*Now let's complete the bottom part of the diamond shape.*

**22.** Repeat step 14.

**23.** Repeat step 13, twice.

**24.** Use cord 12 as knot-bearer and make a row of diagonal double half hitches from right to left, using cords 11–1.

*This completes the bottom of the diamond shape and starts the top of the next diamond.*

**25.** Continue this alternating double diamond pattern (steps 5–24) until you reach one half the desired length of your belt. (Remember that the fringed ends require about a foot [30 cm] on either end.)

**26.** Turn the belt around and continue the pattern on the second half.

**27.** Stop the knotting pattern when the belt, pulled tight, is 1–3 inches (2.5–7.5 cm) shorter than your waist.

*Now, let's make our fringed ends.*

**28.** Use cords 11 and 12, and tie a tight overhand knot around the remaining cords. Secure this knot with clear-drying glue and allow to dry.

**29.** Repeat step 28 with the other end.

**30.** Divide your cords into paired groups and string with randomly spaced beads. Secure the beads with overhand knots and secure the knots with glue. Allow to dry.

**31.** Trim ends.

*Fashion, elegance, sophistication—it's all here in black and white. Freshwater pearls dress up this already alluring ensemble.*

# BLACK AND WHITE BIB NECKLACE AND EARRINGS

DESIGNER: **ELAINE LIEBERMAN**

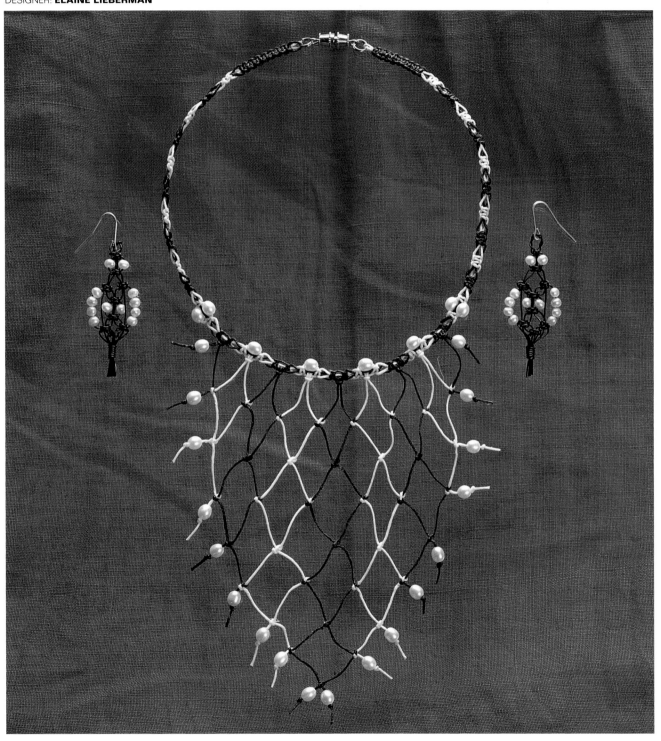

# Necklace

## FINISHED LENGTH
14 inches (35 cm) around. Bib extends approximately 4 inches (10 cm).

## KNOTS USED
Lark's head, square knots with interchanging anchor and knotting cords, half hitch, overhand

## MATERIALS
2 split rings 4-6mm
3-ply black waxed linen
- 1 cord cut 8 feet (240 cm)
- 5 cords cut 3 feet (90 cm) each

3-ply white waxed linen
- 1 cord cut 8 feet (240 cm)
- 4 cords cut 3 feet (90 cm) each

26 semi-round 4 or 5mm freshwater pearls
Barrel clasp

## TOOLS
Measuring tape
Scissors
Macramé work board
T-pins
Chain-nose pliers
Clear-drying glue

## INSTRUCTIONS

**1.** Loop the two 8 foot long (240 cm) cords through a split ring and center. This will give you four working cords of 4 feet (120 cm) each. Secure to your knotting board with a T-pin through the ring.

**2.** Make eight square knots, using the black cords as your knotters and the white cords as your anchor cords.

**3.** Leaving about ⅛ inch (3mm) from your last square knot, switch the positions of your knotting and anchor cords. Make two square knots.

**4.** Repeat step 3 nine times. You will have 10 sets of square knots—five white and five black.

**5.** Using your white cords as knotters, make one square knot.

**6.** String one pearl on each of your knotting (white) cords and make another square knot.

**7.** Using your black cords as knotters, make one square knot.

*Now we will start attaching the bib.*

**8.** Mount one of your black cords onto the two left-hand cords (one white, one black) with a Lark's head knot.

**9.** Repeat step 7.

**10.** Switch the positions of your knotting and anchor cords, and make one square knot.

**11.** String one pearl onto the right hand cord.

**12.** Repeat step 8, using one of your white cords.

**13.** Using your white cords as knotters, make one square knot.

**14.** Repeat steps 7–13 three times.

**15.** Repeat steps 7–9. (All of your cords will now be mounted.)

**16.** Repeat steps 5 and 6.

**17.** Repeat step 3 ten times.

**18.** After your last set of square knots, (white), switch your cords and make four square knots.

**19.** Loop the white cords through the remaining split ring. Fold the ends back toward the last square knots you made. These four white cords will now be your anchor cords.

**20.** Leave enough room between the last square knot you made in step 18 and the split ring, and make four or five more square knots.

**21.** Tie the knotting cords together at the back of the necklace.

**22.** Tie the anchor cords together at the back of the necklace.

**23.** Trim the ends to about ¼ inch (6mm).

**24.** Glue the knots and ends to the back of the necklace. Let dry.

**25.** Attach clasp to each end.

*Now, let's work on our bib. The bib is constructed of eight rows. The cords are joined with half hitches. Be mindful of your spacing, as you knot, and try to keep the open diamond shapes roughly the same size.*

**26.** Pin the necklace to your knotting board, so that it's slightly curved.

**27.** Number your cords 1–18, from left to right.

**28.** About ½ inch (13mm) below the mounting, using cord 8 as your knotting cord and cord 9 as your knot-bearer, make a half hitch. Hold the cords so they form a triangle with the top of the necklace. Make another half hitch, using cord 9 as your knotting cord and cord 8 as your knot-bearer.

**29.** Working from the center outwards, repeat step 28 to join the following cords: 7 and 6; 10 and 11; 5 and 4; 12 and 13; 3 and 2; 14 and 15. Cords 1 and 18 are not used.

*You've just made the first row. You should have eight sets of half hitches.*

**30.** Start row two by joining cords 9 and 10 (both black), then work outward joining the three pairs on either side. You'll have seven sets of half hitches in this row. Cords 2 and 17 are not used.

**31.** Repeat this process for six more rows. The eighth, and last, row will have just cords 9 and 10.

**32.** String a pearl onto the end of each cord. Secure with overhand knots.

**33.** Trim cords and apply a small dab of glue to each knot. Let dry.

# Earrings

## FINISHED LENGTH
Approximately 2 inches (5 cm) long

## KNOTS USED
Square

## MATERIALS
24-gauge black coated copper wire
- 8 pieces cut 18 inches (45 cm) each

24 semi-round 3mm freshwater pearls

2 ear wires

## TOOLS
Measuring tape

Wire cutters

Macramé work board

T-pins

Chain-nose pliers

*The materials given are for the pair of earrings, but the instructions are for one. It's a good idea to make both earrings simultaneously, so you can compare them as you work. Keep them pinned on your knotting board, side-by-side.*

## INSTRUCTIONS

**1.** Join two pieces of wire at their center points, by twisting one around the other three times.

**2.** Place a T-pin under the twists and bend the wires so all four hang down.

**3.** Make one square knot.

**4.** String one pearl onto each knotting cord.

**5.** Repeat step 3.

**6.** Separate your four wires into a left-hand set of two and a right-hand set of two.

**7.** Fold a new piece of wire in half. Using this piece as your knotting wires, make a square knot around the left-hand set of two.

**8.** Repeat step 7, with another piece of wire on the right side.

**9.** Using your four center wires, make a square knot. (Your knots will tend to slide a bit. Use small T-pins to help keep them in place.)

**10.** Repeat steps 4 and 5.

**11.** String four pearls onto your far-left wire and four onto your far-right wire.

**12.** Make a square knot with the four wires on the left and another square knot with the four wires on the right.

**13.** Repeat step 9.

**14.** Bring all of the ends together. Wrap the right-hand wire around the others six times. Bend your wrapping wire back into the group.

**15.** Cut the wires about ¼ inch (6mm) below the wrapped section.

**16.** Attach ear wire.

# EYE-OF-THE-TIGER CHOKER

*This sumptuously simple choker is made with sophisticated soutache and tantilizing tiger's eye beads. Catch the eye of someone special with this purrrfect necklace.*

DESIGNER: **ELAINE LIEBERMAN**

**FINISHED LENGTH**

Approximately 28 inches (70 cm)

**KNOTS USED**

Overhand, square,
diagonal double half hitch

**MATERIALS**

Brown soutache
- 2 cords cut 4½ feet
  (135 cm) each
- 1 cord cut 6 feet (180 cm)

5 standard 1-inch (2.5 cm) head pins

Tiger's eye round beads
- Five 8mm beads
- Five 4mm beads

**TOOLS**

Measuring tape
Scissors
Macramé work board
T-pins
Clear-drying glue
Round-nose pliers

*Soutache is a flat cord. Your work will
have a more professional look if you can
avoid twisting the cord, especially in the
open areas of the choker. If you are a
novice knotter, you might try making
this in #1 rattail first.*

**INSTRUCTIONS**

**1.** Tie your two 4½-foot (135 cm) cords
together using an overhand knot. Make
your knot about a foot (30 cm) from the
ends.

**2.** Secure to your knotting board by
pinning through the overhand knot.
Let's refer to this as cord A.

**3.** Fold your 6-foot (180 cm) cord
unevenly, so that the right side is one
foot (30 cm) longer than the left. Let's
refer to this as cord B.

**4.** Place cord B under cord A. The fold
point of cord B should be just beneath
the overhand knot you tied.

**5.** Make five square knots, using the B
cords as your knotting cords and the A
cords as your anchor cords, or fillers.

**6.** Using your left-hand cord (the
shorter one) as knot-bearer, make a row
of 3 diagonal double half hitches, from
left to right.

**7.** Continuing with the same knot-
bearer, switch directions and make a
row of diagonal double half hitches,
from right to left. Use a T-pin to help
keep your knot-bearer angle sharp and
your knotting even.

**8.** Continue making rows of diagonal
double half hitches, until you've made
14 rows, seven in each direction.

**9.** Make five square knots.

**10.** Tie your knotting cords together
with a tight square knot, in the back of
the choker. Cut the ends, leaving about
a ½ inch (13mm).

**11.** Untie the overhand knot you made
in step 1.

**12.** Cut both ends of the choker about
10 inches (25 cm) from the last square
knots.

**13.** Tie overhand knots, leaving about
a ½-inch (13mm) tail at each end.

**14.** Glue the tight square knot you made
in step 10 and the tail to the back of the
choker.

**15.** Glue the overhand knots and tails
at either end of the choker. Allow to dry.

*Before we can add the beads, let's dis-
tinguish the top of the choker from the
bottom. Seven V shapes (formed by diagonal double half hitches) are revealed
when the choker is laid in the correct
position. We'll add our beads to the bot-
toms of five of these V shapes. We'll leave
the first and last plain.*

**16.** Place one 8mm bead on a head pin
followed by a 4mm bead. Loop head pin
around cord as described on page 13.

**17.** Repeat with the rest of the beads.

# YUPPIE-PUPPY COLLAR AND LEASH

*Turn your Fido into a fashion plate with this Yuppie-Puppy Collar and Leash combo. Rugged and handsome, the choker-style and sturdy polypropylene cord ensure your sense of canine control.*

DESIGNER: **JIM GENTRY**

# Collar

## FINISHED SIZE

1 x 14 inches (2.5 x 35 cm)

## KNOTS USED

Lark's head, square, diagonal double half hitch, vertical Lark's head, overhand

## MATERIALS

2mm braided polypropylene macramé cord:

- 2 gray cords cut 4 yards (3.6 m) each
- 1 dark blue cord cut 4 yards (3.6 m)

2 metal O-rings, 1½-inch (3.8 cm) diameter

## TOOLS

Measuring tape
Scissors
T-pins
Macramé work board
Crochet hook, or heavy yarn needle
Clear-drying glue

## INSTRUCTIONS

*You may, of course, use any color combination you like. However, it will be a bit easier to follow this vertical Lark's head pattern if you stick to just two colors. Make sure you follow the basic color scheme used here.*

**1.** Secure one of the O-rings to your knotting board with T pins.

**2.** Mount your cords to the O-ring, using Lark's head knots. Position them from left to right: blue, gray, gray. Number your cords 1–6, from left to right.

**3.** Tie one square knot using cords 1, 2, and 3. Notice there's just one anchor cord.

**4.** Tie one square knot using cords 4, 5, and 6.

**5.** Tie one square knot using cords 2–5. This time you have two anchor cords.

*Now, you'll make a V shape of diagonal double half hitches below the square knots you just tied.*

**6.** Hold cord 1 diagonally over cords 2 and 3. Keep cord 1 taut, and tie double half hitches with cords 2 and 3.

**7.** Hold cord 6 diagonally over cords 5 and 4. Keep cord 6 taut, and tie double half hitches with cords 5 and 4.

*Now, we'll begin our alternating vertical Lark's head pattern.*

**8.** Tie a vertical Lark's head knot, using cord 1 as your knotting cord and cord 2 as your anchor/filler cord.

**9.** Tie a vertical Lark's head knot, using cord 6 as your knotting cord and cord 5 as your anchor/filler cord.

**10.** Cross cords 3 and 4. (Make an X.) Keep cord 3 under 4.

**11.** Tie a vertical Lark's head knot, using cord 3 as your knotting cord and cord 2 as your anchor/filler cord.

**12.** Tie a vertical Lark's head knot, using cord 4 as your knotting cord and cord 5 as your anchor/filler cord.

**13.** Repeat step 8.

**14.** Repeat step 9.

**15.** Repeat step 10.

**16.** Repeat step 11.

**17.** Repeat step 12.

**18.** Continue knotting in this pattern until you have reached a length of 14 inches (35 cm).

*Now let's attach the second O-ring, finish off the collar, and make the leash.*

**19.** Tie one square knot using cords 1, 2, and 3 (with just one anchor cord).

**20.** Tie one square knot using cords 4, 5, and 6.

**21.** Slip cords 3 and 4 through the O-ring.

**22.** Tie one square knot using cords 2,3,4, and 5. This will secure the O-ring.

**23.** Repeat step 19.

**24.** Repeat step 20.

**25.** Using your crochet hook (or needle), weave cords 1 and 6 back through the side loops created by the knotting pattern.

**26.** Leave each cord on the inside of the collar and secure the ends with overhand knots.

**27.** Trim the ends and coat with glue. Allow to dry.

**28.** Tie an overhand knot with the two cords on the left. Tighten, and trim the end. Repeat with the two cords on the right. Coat with glue and allow to dry thoroughly.

# Leash

### FINISHED SIZE

½ inch x 5 feet (1.25 x 150 cm)

### KNOTS USED

Overhand, square,
double half hitch

### MATERIALS

2mm braided polypropylene
macramé cord:

- 1 gray cord cut 2⅓ yards (2.1 m)
- 1 gray cord cut 7 yards (6.3 m)
- 1 dark blue cord cut 2⅓ yards (2.1 m)
- 1 dark blue cord cut 7 yards (6.3 m)

Metal snap

### TOOLS

Measuring tape

Scissors

Rubber bands

T-pins

Macramé work board

Clear-drying glue

*This sturdy leash is a very simple square knot sennit. Although it's easy, it's important to keep your knotting even and tight. As with the collar, feel free to use whatever colors you like, but do follow the basic color scheme. Notice that we have two long cords (one gray, one blue) and two shorter cords (one gray, one blue). The short cords will be used as the anchor cords, or fillers. The long ones will be our knotting cords. To make knotting easier, this leash is worked from the middle to the hand loop and then from the middle to the metal snap.*

## INSTRUCTIONS

**1.** Find the center point of each cord.

**2.** Tie all the cords together at their center points with an overhand knot.

**3.** To keep your cords manageable, wrap them into butterfly bobbins and secure with rubber bands. Wrap to within a foot (30 cm), or so of the overhand knot. (See page 14 for instructions.)

**4.** Pin your cords through the overhand knot to your knotting board.

**5.** Make sure you have your cords positioned properly—the two short anchor cords on the inside and the two long knotting cords on the outside.

(**NOTE:** *You can use different colored rubber bands on your butterflies to visually distinguish your anchors from your knotters. This makes square knotting so mindless you can watch television, chat on the phone, or even do your homework and make your sennit at the same time. Only experienced knotters should attempt all four at once.*)

**6.** What are you waiting for? Start square knotting. Continue knotting until you're about a foot (30 cm) away from the ends.

*Now let's make the hand loop.*

**7.** Fold the sennit back onto itself for about 6 inches (15 cm).

**8.** Using the same knotting cords you've been using, tie three square knots around the completed sennit and your old anchor cords.

**9.** Trim the old anchor cords just below the third square knot.

**10.** Tie another square knot. There will be no anchor cords.

**11.** Tie your two knotting cords with a tight overhand knot, to secure.

**12.** Trim the ends about ⅛ inch (3mm) from the knot. Coat with glue. Let dry.

*Let's get going on the other half of our leash. I don't know about you, but my dog needs a walk!*

**13.** Untie the overhand knot and resume square knotting, just as before.

**14.** When your sennit is about 5 feet (15 cm) long, bring the cord on the far right across the other three. Hold it perfectly horizontal and taut.

**15.** Make a row of horizontal double half hitches.

*Now it's time to attach our hardware. Your hardware may have a slightly different attachment device...perhaps a swivel ring. You can still follow this procedure.*

**16.** Bring your knotting cords over the metal snap bar and your anchor cords under the bar.

**17.** To secure, make another row of tight horizontal double half hitches, this time from left to right.

**18.** Tie a square knot, using all four cords.

**19.** Tie an overhand knot with the two gray cords and tighten firmly.

**20.** Repeat step 19, using the two blue cords.

**21.** Trim the two overhand knots ⅛ inch (3mm) below the knot and coat ends with glue. Let dry.

*Now, let's get those pooches to the park!*

# FRIENDSHIP CHOKER WITH DANGLE

*These easy-to-make friendship chokers are great as gifts and swell to swap.*
*Customize with the bead, bell, or charm of your choice.*

DESIGNER: **ELAINE LIEBERMAN**

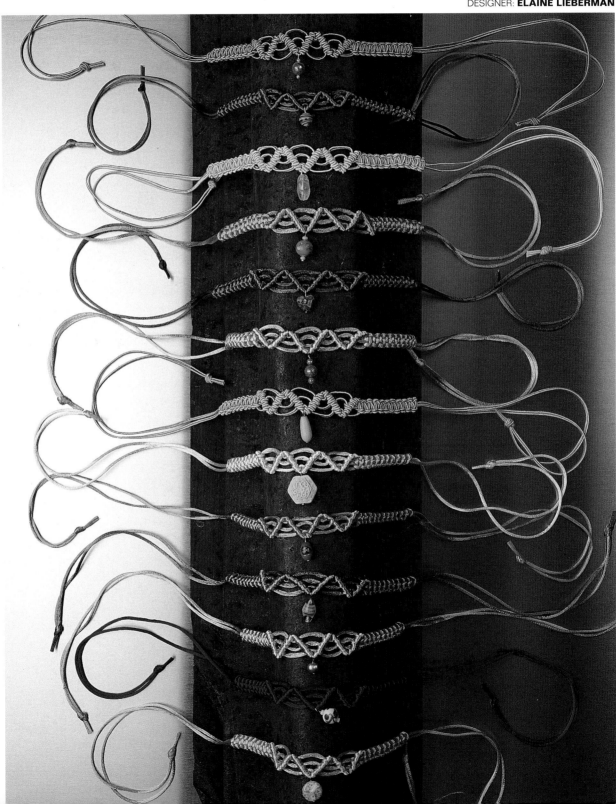

## INSTRUCTIONS

**1.** Tie your two 3½-foot (105 cm) cords together using an overhand knot. Make your knot about a foot (30 cm) from the ends.

**2.** Secure to your knotting board by pinning through the overhand knot. Let's refer to this as cord A.

**3.** Fold your 7-foot (210 cm) cord in half. Let's refer to this as cord B.

**4.** Place cord B under cord A. The center point of cord B should be just beneath the overhand knot you tied.

**5.** Make 10 square knots, using the B cords as your knotting cords and the A cords as your anchor cords, or fillers.

**6.** Using your left-hand cord as knot-bearer, make a row of three diagonal double half hitches, from left to right.

**7.** Continuing with the same knot-bearer, switch directions and make a row of diagonal double half hitches, from right to left.

*Use a T-pin to help keep your knot-bearer angle sharp and your knotting even.*

**8.** Continue making rows of diagonal double half hitches, until you've made six rows, three in each direction.

**9.** Make 10 square knots.

**10.** Tie your knotting cords together with a tight square knot, in the back of the choker. Cut the ends, leaving about ½ inch (13mm).

**11.** Untie the overhand knot you made in step 1.

**12.** Cut both ends of the choker about 10 inches (25 cm) from the last square knots.

**13.** Tie overhand knots, leaving about a ½-inch (13mm) tail at each end.

**14.** Glue the tight square knot and the tail to the back of the choker.

**15.** Glue the overhand knots and tails on either end of the choker. Allow to dry.

**16.** At the base of the middle V formed by the diagonal double half hitches, attach the bead with a head pin as described on page 13.

### FINISHED LENGTH
Approximately 24 inches (60 cm)

### KNOTS USED
Overhand, square,
diagonal double half hitch

### MATERIALS
Rattail #1
- 2 cords cut 3½ feet (105 cm) each
- 1 cord cut 7 feet (210 cm)

1 standard 1-inch (2.5 cm) head pin

One 10mm decorative bead

### TOOLS
Measuring tape

Scissors

Macramé work board

T-pins

Clear-drying glue

Round-nose pliers

# PURPLE PICOT PERFECTION

*Delicate picots, accent beads, and half knot twists frame the bold bead centerpiece of this perfectly simple necklace.*

DESIGNER: **PAT THIBODEAUX**

## FINISHED LENGTH

Approximately 22 inches (55 cm)

## KNOTS USED

Overhand, square, half

## MATERIALS

7-ply waxed linen

- 6 cords cut 60 inches (150 cm) each
- 2 cords cut 36 inches (90 cm) each

1 large and 2 medium matching beads—holes must accommodate all 8 cords

2 medium/small accent beads

12 small accent beads

1 metal bead

## TOOLS

Measuring tape

Scissors

Macramé work board

T-pins or tape

**NOTE:** *This necklace is started in the middle, with the bold bead centerpiece. One side is knotted and completed before beginning the second side.*

## INSTRUCTIONS

**1.** Find the center point of all eight cords. The 60-inch (150 cm) cords will be much longer at each end than the 36-inch (90 cm) cords. String your large bead to the center point of all eight cords. Tie an overhand knot on either side of the bead to secure.

**2.** String a medium bead on either side of the overhand knots you just made. Follow with overhand knots to secure.

**3.** You now have six 30-inch (75 cm) cords and two 18-inch (45 cm) cords. The two short cords will be your anchor cords and the six long cords will become the knotting cords, with three on either side.

**4.** String one small accent bead on the right anchor cord and two accent beads on the left anchor cord. Stagger as shown.

**5.** Using your six knotting cords, tie a very loose square knot below the beads. Form the picots by fanning the knotting cords out. (Use tape or T-pins to help shape.) Tighten your square knot only after you're satisfied with the appearance of the picots.

**6.** String a medium/small accent bead onto the anchor cords.

**7.** Tie a very loose square knot below the bead you just strung. Leave a little extra cord, to make your picots slightly larger than the previous set. Tighten the knot, when the loops are to your liking.

**8.** Repeat step 4.

**9.** Tie a very loose overhand knot with all eight cords. Spread out your knotting cords to form picots. Tighten knot.

**10.** Tie 26 half knots. Your two short cords are still used as the anchors, and your six longer cords are the knotting cords—three on each side. (After the third or fourth knot, your sennit will begin to naturally twist.)

**11.** Tie an overhand knot. All the cords should be about the same length now. If necessary, trim up the ends to make even.

**12.** Take four cords and twist them tightly together in a clockwise direction. Tape the end, or hold firmly. Repeat with the other four cords. Thread the metal bead onto the ends and secure with an overhand knot.

**13.** These two cords will begin to twist together counterclockwise, naturally. Twist them together tightly, by hand, to form a "rope."

**14.** This completes side one of the necklace. Move to the other side and repeat steps 4 through 12. Except: in step 4, reverse the position of the small accent beads. In step 12, omit the metal bead and finish with just the overhand knot.

**15.** To tie the necklace, make an opening for the metal bead by separating the two twisted cords below the overhand knot.

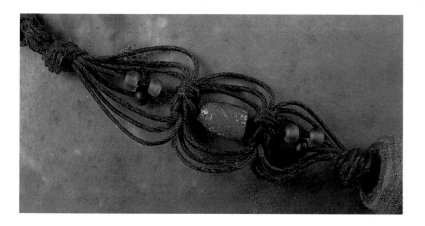

# WAIST KNOT— WANT KNOT BELT

*What a great way to recycle those old buckles from the belts you no longer wear! This handsome belt's a cinch.*

DESIGNER: **ELAINE LIEBERMAN**

### FINISHED SIZE

Make to fit

(Waist measurement + 8 inches (20 cm), x 9 + 2 feet (60 cm) will make a belt to fit the waist of your choice.)

### KNOTS USED

Lark's head, double half hitches, square

### MATERIALS

Seine twine—size 21
- 6 cords cut to your specifications

1 favorite buckle

Sewing thread to match twine

### TOOLS

Measuring tape

Scissors

Rubber bands

Macramé work board

T-pins

Sewing needle

## INSTRUCTIONS

**1.** Fold cords in half and mount to the buckle with Lark's head knots.

**2.** Wrap your excess cords into butterfly bobbins, as described on page 14.

**3.** Number your cords 1–12, from left to right.

**4.** Using cord 1 as knot-bearer, make one row of horizontal double half hitches from left to right, then make another row from right to left.

**5.** Using cord 1 as knot-bearer, make one row of diagonal double half hitches working from left to right. Keep your knot-bearer taut.

**6.** Repeat step 5, twice (for three rows of diagonal double half hitches).

**7.** Make three square knots with cords 1–4.

**8.** Make two square knots with cords 5–8.

**9.** Make one square knot with cords 9–12.

**10.** Make one square knot with cords 3–6.

**11.** Make one square knot with cords 7–10.

**12.** Make one square knot with cords 1–4.

**13.** Repeat step 8.

**14.** Make three square knots with cords 9–12.

**15.** Repeat steps 5–14 until your belt is 2 inches (5 cm) shorter than the desired finished length.

**16.** Repeat steps 5 and 6.

**17.** Repeat step 12.

**18.** Using cord 6 as your knot-bearer, make a row of diagonal double half hitches from left to right.

**19.** Make one square knot with cords 5–8.

**20.** Repeat step 10.

**21.** Repeat step 11.

**22.** Repeat step 19.

**23.** Using cord 1 as knot-bearer, make a row of five diagonal double half hitches from left to right.

**24.** Using cord 12 as knot-bearer, make a row of five diagonal double half hitches from right to left.

**25.** Repeat step 23.

**26.** Repeat step 24.

**27.** Using cord 7 as your knot-bearer, make one double half hitch with cord 6.

**28.** Bring the cords to the back of your belt and trim to ¼ inch (6mm).

**29.** Sew the ends to the back of the belt. Sew cords 6 and 7 to the sides of the belt, so they don't show in the center open space. (Sewing the ends provides a much more durable finish than gluing.)

# STAR-SPANGLED DANGLE BANGLE

*Declare your independence from the ordinary with this patriotic bracelet. Festive and fun and oh so easy to make!*

DESIGNER: **PAT THIBODEAUX**

## FINISHED LENGTH

Approximately 8½ inches (21 cm)

## KNOTS USED

Square, overhand, Josephine, Lark's head

## MATERIALS

4-ply waxed linen
- 8 cords cut 22 inches (55 cm) each
- 3 cords cut 4 inches (10 cm) each

1 large and 2 medium matching glass tube beads

6 star accent beads (8 mm)

1 metal (flying saucer shaped) bead for clasp

## TOOLS

Measuring tape

Scissors

Macramé work board

T-pins

Tape

**NOTE**: *This bracelet is started in the middle, with the large tube bead. Since this is such an easy and short piece, let's knot the two sides simultaneously. Before finishing off the ends, try the bracelet on and adjust the size, if needed.*

## INSTRUCTIONS

**1.** Place the eight cords on your work board. Make them parallel and even. Find and mark the center point of the cords, and secure to the board with tape. Number your cords from left to right, 1–8.

**2.** String your large tube bead to the center point of cords 3, 4, 5, and 6.

**3.** Make one square knot just below the bead using cords 1, 2, 7, and 8 as your knotting cords.

**4.** Untape your cords and make another square knot just above the bead using the same knotting cords as before. Fan the knotting cords out to form picots, as pictured.

**5.** String the two medium tube beads onto cords 3, 4, 5, and 6, as shown.

**6.** Follow the medium tube beads with overhand knots. Again, fan out your cords to form picots, as shown.

**7.** Follow the overhand knots with Josephine knots. Make sure your cords are straight and flat before tying your Josephine knots.

**8.** Make overhand knots at the end of the Josephine knots.

**9.** Take four cords and twist them tightly together in a clockwise direction. Tape the end, or hold firmly. Repeat with the other four cords. Thread the metal (flying saucer shaped) bead onto the two sets of twisted cord. Tie an overhand knot and trim.

**10.** The two cords you just formed will begin to twist together counterclockwise, naturally. Twist them together tightly, by hand, to form a "rope."

**11.** Repeat steps 9 and 10, but omit the metal bead and finish with just the overhand knot.

**12.** To tie the bracelet, make an opening for the metal bead by separating the two twisted cords. Insert the bead and retwist to secure.

*And now, for the finishing touch…
let's add the stars.*

**13.** String two stars onto each of the three remaining cords. Secure with overhand knots.

**14.** Mount cords with Lark's head knots onto the outer picots, as shown. Make your cords slightly uneven.

# ESSENTIAL OIL NECKLACE

*Wear your favorite scent in a whole new way. A square knot strap and alternating square knot bottle cover are combined with a delightful assortment of beads, charms, and bells.*

DESIGNER: **JENNIFER LAKE**

## FINISHED LENGTH

Approximately 17 inches (42.5 cm)

## KNOTS USED

Lark's head, overhand,
half knot, square

## MATERIALS

1 small bottle, ¼ ounce (7.5 ml)

.5mm polished hemp cord

- 2 cords cut 1½ yards
  (1.3 m) each

.5mm hemp beading yarn

- 2 cords cut 3½ yards
  (3 m) each
- 12 cords cut 2 feet
  (60 cm) each

An assortment of beads,
charms, and bells

## TOOLS

Measuring tape
Scissors
T-pins
Clipboard
Clear-drying glue

*This little bottle is a bit awkward to work with. Try securing it to a clipboard, or hanging it from a fixture and work standing up. You'll be knotting in the round, so you might want to wind your cords into butterfly bobbins to keep things manageable (see page 14). Make yourself comfortable! Use a clean empty bottle with the cap removed.*

## INSTRUCTIONS

**1.** Take one of the polished hemp cords and fold it in half. Loop it around the top of the bottle and secure with a loose overhand knot.

**2.** Take the other polished hemp cord and fold it in half. Loop it around the top of the bottle, facing the opposite direction. Secure with a loose overhand knot.

*These two cords will serve as holding cords and as our straps.*

**3.** Mount the 12 cords of beading yarn, using Lark's head knots, to the holding cords. Mount six on one side of the bottle and six on the other. You now have 24 working cords.

**4.** To tighten the strap cords, untie your loose overhand knot and tie a very tight half knot (there are no anchors/fillers). Follow this half knot with a tight overhand knot.

**5.** Repeat on the other side.

*We're ready to begin our alternating square knotting around the bottle. Move the strap cords up out of your way. To keep it simple, let's number our cords from 1–24.*

**6.** Using groups of four cords, make your first row of square knots. (Your first knot will use cords 1, 2, 3, and 4. Cords 2 and 3 are your anchors/fillers, and 1 and 4 are your knotting cords.) Your first row will have six square knots.

**7.** Using groups of four cords, make a second row of square knots. (Your first knot will use cords 3, 4, 5, and 6. Cords 4 and 5 are your anchors/fillers, and 3 and 6 are your knotting cords.) The first and last two cords are omitted.

**8.** Continue with this alternating square knot pattern. Keep your knotting even, open, and stretch it down as you work. Knot one row past the bottom of the bottle. You will have about 10 rows of alternating square knots.

**9.** Make an overhand knot with all 24 cords. Pull each cord individually to tighten the knot.

**10.** Add charms, beads, and bells to the cords and secure with overhand knots. Use a little clear-drying glue to secure your knots.

**11.** Trim fringe to the length you desire.

*Now, let's finish the straps. We'll finish one strap first, then repeat our steps and complete the other.*

**12.** Take one of your remaining two cords and fold it in half. Tie it around one of the strap cords with a tight half knot.

**13.** Tie three tight square knots, using the new cords as your knotting cords and the original strap cords as your anchors.

**14.** Continue making square knots, leaving about a ¼-inch (6mm) space between the knots.

**15.** Continue knotting until you reach the desired length of your necklace.

**16.** Repeat steps 12–15 to finish the other strap.

**17.** Tie the straps together with a very tight overhand knot. Trim and coat with clear-drying glue to secure knot. Let dry.

# TRUE BLUE BUCKAROO HAT BAND

*Here's a handy hat trick. Spiff up your sombrero, please your panama, and freshen your fedora—all with this easy, two-tone knotted band. It's not just for cowboys any more.*

DESIGNER: **JIM GENTRY**

## FINISHED SIZE

28 inches (70 cm) total length

## KNOTS USED

Overhand, square, diagonal double half hitch

## MATERIALS

100% Rayon yarn (rust and dark gold):

- 4 rust cords cut 3 yards (2.7 m) each
- 4 dark gold cords cut 3 yards (2.7 m) each

## TOOLS

Measuring tape

Scissors

T-pins

Macramé work board

*Choose whatever type of fiber and color that suits your mood and your particular hat. As your knotting progresses, put the band on your hat and adjust for your specific length, as needed. To make knotting easier, this hatband is worked from the middle to one end and then from the middle to the other end.*

## INSTRUCTIONS

**1.** Find the center point of each cord.

**2.** Tie all the cords together at their center points, using an overhand knot.

**3.** To keep your cords manageable, wrap them into butterfly bobbins and secure with rubber bands. Wrap to within a foot (30 cm) or so of the overhand knot. (See page 14 for instructions.)

**4.** Pin your cords through the overhand knot to your knotting board.

**5.** Divide your cords into two groups—color A on the left, color B on the right.

**6.** Tie eight square knots with the four cords in color A.

**7.** Tie eight square knots with the four cords in color B.

*The square knot sennits are the first part of this two-part design. For the next part, we're going to join our two sennits, using diagonal double half hitches. It's important to keep your hitches tight and even.*

**8.** Number your cords, from left to right, 1–8.

**9.** Use cord 5 as your knot-bearer and tie a row of diagonal double half hitches, working from right to left.

**10.** Repeat step 9, using cord 6 as your knot-bearer.

**11.** Repeat step 9, using cord 7 as your knot-bearer.

**12.** Repeat step 9, using cord 8 as your knot-bearer.

*That completes the second part of the design. Notice that our colors have changed sides.*

**13.** Make two more square knot sennits, with eight knots in each.

**14.** Join the sennits again with diagonal double half hitches, as you did in steps 8–12.

**15.** Repeat this two-part pattern (sennits, then double half hitches), until you reach the desired length of your hatband. You must end with a diagonal double half hitch section on either end. (The design, as shown, has 16 sennit sections and 17 double half hitch sections.)

*Now, let's finish the ends of the band. First, we need to reduce the number of cords we're using. Instead of making square knots, after our last diagonal double half hitch section, we're going to make two more rows of gathering double half hitches.*

**16.** Use cord 1 as your knot-bearer; hold it diagonal and taut. Make a double half hitch with cord 2.

**17.** Use cords 1 and 2 as your knot-bearer, and make a double half hitch with cord 3.

**18.** Use cords 1, 2, and 3 as your knot-bearer and make a double half hitch with cord 4.

**19.** Repeat this process of gathering with cords 8–5, working right to left.

**20.** Tie a square knot, using cords 1 and 8 as your knotting cords, and 2–7 as your anchor or filler cords.

**21.** Cut out 4 cords (2 of each color) right below the square knot you just tied.

**22.** Tie 8 square knots.

**23.** Repeat steps 16–22 to finish the other end of the band.

**24.** Join the ends together with a square knot and trim. Happy Trails!

# KNOT NATURAL NECKLACE AND EARRINGS

*This fresh earth-tone ensemble features nutural waxed linen and rustic looking beads. Cords are organically incorporated in these elegant pieces.*

DESIGNER: **ELAINE LIEBERMAN**

# Necklace

### FINISHED LENGTH

Approximately 11 inches (27.5cm). To make a longer necklace, cut your cords 1 foot (30 cm) longer, per 3½ inches (8.75 cm) of additional desired length.

### KNOTS USED

Square, double half hitch, overhand

### MATERIALS

4-ply natural color waxed linen:
- 6 cords cut 7 feet (210 cm) each

56 rust seed beads (size 8)

11 brown (matte finish) e-beads

16 ivory e-beads

2 jump rings (4mm)

1 barrel clasp

### TOOLS

Measuring tape

Scissors

Macramé work board

T-pins

Clear-drying glue

Chain-nose pliers

### INSTRUCTIONS

*This necklace is started at the bottom.*

**1.** String 11 beads onto one of your six cords in the following order: 1 seed bead, 1 e-bead, 1 seed bead, 1 ivory e-bead, 1 seed bead, 1 e-bead, 1 seed bead, 1 ivory e-bead, 1 seed bead, 1 e-bead, 1 seed bead. Fold the cord in half with the beads centered at the top. These two cords will be your anchor cords.

**2.** Fold another cord in half and position it behind the beaded cord. The fold point should be just beneath the loop of beads. These will be your knotting cords.

**3.** Make two square knots. Secure your work to the knotting board with T-pins, and slide the knots up close to the beads.

**4.** Switch your anchor cords with your knotting cords. Leave about ¼ inch (6mm) between the bottom of your last square knot and the top of the next.

**5.** Make one square knot.

**6.** On each of your knotting cords, string 1 seed bead, 1 ivory e-bead, and 1 seed bead.

**7.** Repeat step 5.

**8.** Repeat step 4.

**9.** Make two square knots.

*Now, it's time to add our remaining cords.*

**10.** On a new cord, string 1 seed bead, 1 ivory e-bead, and 1 seed bead. Fold the cord in half with the beads centered at the top. These two cords will be your anchor cords.

**11.** Add another (knotting) cord and make two square knots, as in steps 2 and 3.

**12.** Repeat steps 10 and 11 with your two remaining cords.

**13.** Place your new cords on either side of the original. The last pair of square knots on each group should line up perfectly. Secure with more T-pins.

*At this point, let's number our cords, from left to right, 1–12.*

**14.** Make one square knot with cords 3–6. Make another square knot with cords 7–10.

**15.** Using cord 1 as your knot-bearer, make a row of 5 diagonal double half hitches, from left to right.

**16.** Using cord 12 as your knot-bearer, make a row of 5 diagonal double half hitches, from right to left.

**17.** String a seed bead onto cords 1, 3, 5, 8, 10, and 12.

**18.** Repeat steps 15 and 16.

**19.** Make a square knot with cords 5–8.

**20.** String a brown e-bead on cords 5 and 8.

**21.** Repeat step 19.

**22.** Repeat step 20.

**23.** Repeat step 19.

24. Make one square knot using cords 2, 3, and 4, and one square knot using cords 9, 10, and 11. (Note: there's only one anchor cord.)

**25.** Make a square knot using cords 9, 10, and 11. (You have just one anchor cord.)

**26.** On cords 1 and 12, string: 2 seed beads, 1 ivory e-bead, 1 seed bead, 1 brown e-bead, 1 seed bead, 1 ivory e-bead, and 2 seed beads.

**27.** Repeat steps 15 and 16. (Make your double half hitches close enough to the square knots, so the knot-bearers will have rounded shapes.)

**28.** String a brown e-bead on cords 5 and 8.

**29.** Using cord 6 as your knot-bearer, make a row of 5 diagonal double half hitches, from right to left. Repeat on the right side using cord 7 as your knot-bearer. Work from left to right.

**30.** Using cords 4, 5, and 6, make four square knots. You have just one anchor cord.

**31.** Using cord 1 as your knot-bearer, make a row of 5 diagonal double half hitches, from left to right.

**32.** On cord 1 (remember it's the position, not the actual cord) string: 2 seed beads, 1 ivory e-bead and 2 seed beads.

**33.** Using cord 6 as your knot-bearer, make a row of 5 diagonal double half hitches, from right to left.

**34.** Repeat steps 31 and 33.

**35.** Repeat step 32, using cord 6.

**36.** Repeat steps 31, 33 and 31 again.

**37.** Repeat step 32.

**38.** Repeat step 33.

**39.** Repeat step 30.

**40.** Repeat steps 31, 33, and 31 again. (Make a tighter angle with your last row of diagonal double half hitches.)

**41.** Using cords 1, 2, and 3, make three square knots.

**42.** Using cords 4, 5, and 6, make two square knots.

**43.** Using cords 2, 3, and 4, make one square knot.

**44.** Repeat steps 41 and 42.

**45.** Repeat step 33.

**46.** Using cord 1 as knot-bearer, make a row of 3 double half hitches with cords 2, 4, and 6. Move the cords you skipped (3 and 5) out of your way.

**47.** Make two square knots with cords 1, 2, 4, and 6.

**48.** Switch your anchor cords with your knotting cords. Leave about ¼ inch (6mm) between the bottom of your last square knot and the top of the next. Make two square knots.

**49.** Repeat step 48 three times. You now have five sets of square knots.

**50.** Switch your cords one last time and make four square knots.

**51.** Fold your anchor cords around a jump ring from the front to back.

**52.** Leave just enough room between the last square knot you made and the jump ring, to make four more square knots. By folding your anchor cords back toward your knotting, you have doubled your cords.

**53.** Use your original anchor cords as anchors and your two new cords as knotting cords, and make four more square knots.

**54.** Firmly tie your new knotting cords together, with an overhand knot, at the back of the necklace.

**55.** Tie the ends of your anchor cords together, with a half knot, at the back of the necklace.

**56.** Tie cords 3 and 5 (from step 46) the same.

**57.** Trim all cords to ¼ inch (6mm).

**58.** Glue the knots and ends to the back of the necklace. Allow to dry

**59.** Add the clasp.

**60.** Repeat steps 30–59 on the right side (with cords 7–12) to complete the necklace. (Repeat steps in reverse, to create a mirror image of the left side.)

# Earrings

**FINISHED LENGTH**

Approximately 2½ inches
(6 cm) long

**KNOTS USED**

Double half hitch, square

**MATERIALS**

4-ply natural color waxed linen:
- 12 cords cut 3 feet
  (90 cm) each

44 rust seed beads (size 8)

16 brown (matte finish) e-beads

12 ivory e-beads

1 pair of ear wires

**TOOLS**

Measuring tape

Scissors

Macramé work board

T-pins

Clear-drying glue

Chain-nose pliers

*Materials are given for the pair of
earrings; instructions are for one.*

## INSTRUCTIONS

**1.** Fold one cord in half. Place a T-pin under the center. These will be your knotting cords.

**2.** Fold another cord in half and secure one side to your knotting board. Place this cord over the first one. This cord will be your knot-bearer.

**3.** Make a double half hitch with your knotting cord onto your knot-bearer.

**4.** Leave a small loop in the knot-bearer (the ear wire will go here) and make another double half hitch on the other side.

**5.** Place the center of another cord behind your knot-bearer, to the left of the knots you just made. Make a double half hitch with this cord to the left and then to the right.

**6.** Repeat step 5.

**7.** Add your remaining two cords in similar fashion, on the right side. Let's number your cords from left to right, 1–12.

**8.** Make a square knot with cords 5–8.

**9.** String a brown e-bead onto cord 5 and cord 8, and make another square knot.

**10.** Repeat step 9.

**11.** Make a square knot using cords 2, 3, and 4.

**12.** Make a square knot using cords 9, 10, and 11.

**13.** On cord 1, string two seed beads, 1 ivory e-bead, and 2 more seed beads.

**14.** Repeat step 13, using cord 12.

**15.** Using cords 6 and 7 as knot-bearers, make rows of diagonal double half hitches in each direction.

**16.** String a seed bead onto cords 1, 3, 5, 8, 10, and 12.

**17.** Repeat step 15.

**18.** Make a square knot with cords 3–6.

**19.** Make a square knot with cords 7–10.

**20.** Repeat step 8, twice.

**21.** Switch your knotting and anchor cords, leave about ¼ inch (6mm) and make two more square knots.

**22.** String 2 seed beads, 1 ivory e-bead, and 2 more seed beads onto cords 5 and 8.

**23.** Make two more square knots with cords 5–8.

**24.** Make two square knots with cords 1–4.

**25.** String one e-bead onto cord 1 and cord 4.

**26.** Repeat step 24.

**27.** String one ivory bead onto cords 2 and 3.

**28.** Make one square knot.

**29.** Repeat steps 24–28, using cords 9–12 on the right side of the earring.

**30.** To finish off the ends of the three sections, bring the right-hand cord from each square knot around the other cords and through the loop it forms.

**31.** Tighten with the knot placed at the back of the earring.

**32.** Trim the cords ¼ inch (6mm) below the knots.

**33.** Glue the bottom of each section and let dry.

**34.** Attach ear wires.

# ENCHANTING AMULET BAG

*This alluring two-color amulet bag is amazingly easy to make, and what a bewitching way to keep all your favorite gewgaws, secret trinkets, and lucky charms close to your heart.*

DESIGNER: **JANE OLSON**

## FINISHED LENGTH

Approximately 24 inches
(60 cm), including strap

Bag is 2 x 2 inches (5 x 5 cm)

## KNOTS USED

Lark's head, overhand, vertical
double half hitch, half knot

## MATERIALS

Cotton warp thread or heavy
crochet thread

- 4 cords cut 3½ yards (3 m)
  each (color A, blue shown)
- 14 cords cut 24 inches
  (60 cm) each (color B,
  brown shown)
- 6 more cords cut 1½ yards
  (1.35 m) of each color

An assortment of size 6 seed
beads

## TOOLS

Measuring tape

Scissors

Macramé work board

Straight pins

Tape

Needle and matching thread

*Beads may be added to the bag, as
desired. Use a half hitch (not a double)
under the bead to secure. Before beginning each vertical double half hitch,
make sure to pull the knotting cord taut
under the knot-bearer.*

## INSTRUCTIONS

**1.** Find and mark the center points of
your four long cords. These will serve
as your holding cords. Loosely tape
the cords across the top of your knotting board.

**2.** Mount the 14 short cords onto the
center of the long holding cords using
Lark's head knots. This gives you 28
working cords. Use straight pins to hold
work firmly in place.

**3.** Use one of the 1½ yard (1.35 m) color
A cords as your first knotting cord. Tape
one end to the left side of your work
board. Leave about a 5-inch (12.5 cm)
tail. Begin vertical double half hitching
with this cord from left to right, over
each of the 28 knot-bearers. Hitch back
from right to left, and include the tail
with the last knot-bearer. Put the knotting cord aside, out of your way.

**4.** Use one of the 1½ yard (1.35 m) color
B cords as your next knotting cord. Tape
one end to the right side of your work
board. Leave about a 5-inch (12.5 cm)
tail. Knot across from right to left;
include cord A and tail in the last knot.
Knot back to the right, then about
halfway back to the left.

**5.** Use cord A to vertical double half hitch from left to right, until you meet cord B.

**6.** For the next row, cross your cords. Knot with cord A to the right and cord B to the left.

**7.** Add new cords and repeat until you reach the top fold line, at about 4 inches (10 cm). Tails may be trimmed when covered by ½ inch (13mm) of knotting.

**8.** Knot one more row.

**9.** For the next five rows, knot over two knot-bearers, keeping the same color pattern. Pull the knot-bearers tighter together. This will cause the flap to become slightly rounded.

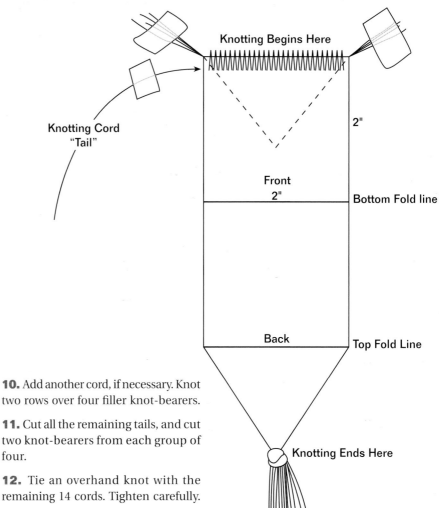

**10.** Add another cord, if necessary. Knot two rows over four filler knot-bearers.

**11.** Cut all the remaining tails, and cut two knot-bearers from each group of four.

**12.** Tie an overhand knot with the remaining 14 cords. Tighten carefully.

**13.** Using your long holding cords, make a 9-inch (22.5 cm) half knot sennit on each side. Switch your knotting and anchor cords, and continue the half knot sennits for an additional 9 inches (22.5 cm) or whatever length you prefer.

**14.** Tie ends together with an overhand knot. Leave about 2 inches (5 cm), and add beads. Secure with overhand knots and trim.

**15.** Sew up the sides of the bag with needle and matching thread.

**16.** Add beads to the fringe on the flap and secure with overhand knots.

DESIGNER: **TRAVIS WALDRON**

# TAKE TWO EARRINGS AND CALL ME IN THE MORNING

*Simple square knots and a few basic beads...it's the perfect remedy for the jewelry blues. These easy wire earrings are good for what ails you and so simple you just might get hooked.*

## FINISHED LENGTH

Approximately
2 inches (5 cm)

## KNOTS USED

Lark's head, square

## MATERIALS

28-gauge copper wire
- 4 pieces cut
  12 inches (30 cm)
  each
2 ear wires
4 copper oval beads
(3 x 6 mm)
4 imitation pearl beads
(4mm)

## TOOLS

Measuring tape
Wire cutters
Macramé work board
T-pins
Nail file

## INSTRUCTIONS

**1.** Find the center points of two pieces of wire and mount them to an ear wire using Lark's head knots. Secure to your knotting board. Number your wires, from left to right, 1–4.

**2.** Make two square knots. Leave about ½ inch (13mm) between your mounting and your first square knot.

**3.** Slide a pearl bead onto wires 2 and 3.

**4.** Make two more square knots.

**5.** Slide one copper bead onto wires 1 and 2 and one bead onto wires 3 and 4. Leave about ¼ inch (6mm) between your last square knot and the copper beads.

**6.** Repeat step 3.

**7.** Repeat step 4.

**8.** Trim wires close to your last square knot and gently file until the ends are no longer sharp.

*The materials given are for the pair of earrings, but the instructions are for one. It's a good idea to make both earrings simultaneously, so you can compare them as you work. Keep them pinned on your knotting board, side-by-side. Why not pair these up with the wire ring on page 102?*

# BEST-SELLER BOOKMARK

*What a handsome gift this would make for your favorite bibliophile. The beautiful pattern is brought to life with rows of alternating diagonal double half hitches.*

DESIGNER: **JIM GENTRY**

**FINISHED LENGTH**
Approximately ⅞ inch (2.2 cm) wide and 8½ inches (21 cm) long

**KNOTS USED**
Overhand, diagonal double half hitch, square

**MATERIALS**
Embroidery floss, cut all cords 36 inches (90 cm) long
- 6 cords of rust
- 4 cords of dark blue
- 6 cords of green
- 8 cords of tan
- 4 cords of yellow

**TOOLS**
Measuring tape
Scissors
Macramé work board
T-pins
Cross-stitch or tapestry needle

*This bookmark is begun in the center. Alternating double half hitches create the woven-like appearance of this piece.*

## INSTRUCTIONS

**1.** Divide cords into two groups of 14 cords each: Group A—6 rust, 6 green, and 2 dark blue; Group B—2 dark blue, 4 yellow, and 8 tan.

**2.** Tie overhand knots at the center points of each group of cords.

**3.** Secure group A to your knotting board with a T-pin through the overhand knot.

**4.** Secure group B the same way, about ¼ inch (6mm) to the right of group A.

*Let's review the order and use of our cords. We have 28 cords, but we're going to double them up and use them as if there were 14. So, from left to right, your double strands will be R, R, R, G, G, G, DB, DB, Y, Y, T, T, T, T. To simplify, we will refer to each double strand as one cord. Let's number the cords 1–14, from left to right. We'll start our first row of knotting about an inch (2.5 cm) below the overhand knots. We will work from left to right first, then back from right to left. This first row will have seven knots.*

**5.** Use cord 1 as your knot-bearer, and tie one diagonal double half hitch with cord 2.

**6.** Use cord 3 as your knot-bearer, and tie one diagonal double half hitch with cord 4.

**7.** Use cord 5 as your knot-bearer, and tie one diagonal double half hitch with cord 6.

**8.** Continue this pattern all the way across. (Your last knot will be made with cord 14.)

*Now we'll start the second (alternating) row. This row will have six knots. We will omit cords 1 and 14.*

**9.** Use cord 13 as your knot-bearer, and tie one diagonal double half hitch with cord 12.

**10.** Use cord 11 as your knot-bearer, and tie one diagonal double half hitch with cord 10.

**11.** Use cord 9 as your knot-bearer, and tie one diagonal double half hitch with cord 8.

**12.** Continue this pattern all the way across. (Your last knot will be made with cord 2.)

**13.** Repeat steps 5–8.

**14.** Repeat steps 9–12.

**15.** Knot in this manner for about 3 inches (7.5 cm).

**16.** Reposition your work and continue knotting on the other side. Knot for about 2 more inches (5 cm), or until the entire length is about 5 inches (12.5 cm).

*Now, we need to bring our ends to a point, or taper them. Start this after you've made a row with six knots in it.*

**17.** Use cord 3 as your knot-bearer, and tie one diagonal double half hitch with cord 4.

**18.** Repeat step 17, using cords 5 and 6.

**19.** Repeat step 17, using cords 7 and 8.

**20.** Repeat step 17, using cords 9 and 10.

**21.** Repeat step 17, using cords 11 and 12.

**22.** Knot another row from right to left, with cords 11–4.

**23.** Knot another row from left to right, with cords 5–10.

**24.** Knot another row from right to left, with cords 9–6.

**25.** Knot another row from left to right, with cords 7 and 8.

**26.** Repeat steps 17–25 on the other end of the bookmark.

*Now, we'll bring all of our cords together so we can make a tassel.*

**27.** Use cord 1 as your knot-bearer, and tie one diagonal double half hitch with cord 2.

**28.** Use cords 1 and 2 as your knot-bearer, and tie one diagonal double half hitch with cord 3.

**29.** Use cords 1, 2, and 3 as your knot bearer, and tie one diagonal double half hitch with cord 4.

**30.** Continue in this manner until you come to a point. Cord 7 will be the last cord you use.

**31.** Repeat steps 27–30 using cords 14–8.

**32.** Repeat steps 27–31 on the other end of the bookmark.

*Now we need to secure our tassel end. We'll do this with square knots.*

**33.** Use cords 7 and 8 as your knotting cords, and make three to four tight square knots around the remaining cords.

**34.** Using your needle, thread each of your knotting cords down into the knot. Trim the ends.

**35.** Finally, trim the ends of your tassel.

**36.** Repeat steps 33–35 on the other end of the bookmark.

# BLUE BEAUTY SHOULDER BAG

*When you stroll down macramé memory lane, don't forget to take along this classic knotted beauty! This stylish square knot bag is made with rugged polypropylene cord and is nearly impossible to wear out. All you need now are sensible shoes!*

DESIGNER: **IRMA BIEGELMAN**

## INSTRUCTIONS

*Making the shoulder bag body*

**1.** Secure holding cord to macramé board with T-pins.

**2.** Fold the 30 cords in half and mount to the holding cord with Lark's head knots.

**3.** Number your cords 1 through 60, from left to right.

**4.** Make the first row by tying 15 square knots. Use four cords for each knot, and work from left to right. Make these knots as close to the holding cord as possible.

**5.** Make the second row of square knots using cords 3–58. You will not use the first two cords and the last two cords. This row will have 14 square knots.

**6.** Repeat step 4. Keep your first and last knots perfectly horizontal. Later, we'll use these side loops to attach the strap to the body of the bag.

**7.** Repeat step 5.

**8.** Continue making rows of alternating square knots until the piece measures 28 inches (70 cm) long, or you have about 81 rows. End with a row of 15 square knots. (The length varies a bit depending on how tight you make your knots.)

*Now, we'll start to shape the flap. This requires eight more rows of square knots, but we're going to leave the first and last two cords of each row free.*

**9.** Make your first row using cords 3–58.

**10.** Your second row of the flap will use cords 5–56. Your third row will use cords 7–54. Your fourth row: 9–52, and so on. Your final row will use cords 17–44 and will have seven square knots in it.

*Now, let's make the Double Hitched edge. First we'll use cord 1 as our knot-bearer and hitch our way (from left to right) all the way across. Then we'll use cord 60 as our knot-bearer and hitch our way (from right to left) back. Ready, set, knot!*

**11.** Use cord 1 as your knot-bearer and tie diagonal double half hitches with cords 2–16. Keep the knot-bearer, taut and your hitches snug against the square knots.

**12.** Switch to single half hitches for cords 17–44. (This is the last row of square knots you made in step 10.) Make sure to keep your knot-bearer perfectly horizontal for this section.

**13.** Resume your diagonal double half hitching, working up to the end of the right side. Remember to keep your knots tight and even.

**14.** Now, use cord 60 as your knot-bearer, and make a second hitched edge. You'll do just what you did in steps 11–13, only now you're working from right to left.

**15.** With a crochet hook, pull all hanging cords to the back of the piece and draw through back loops for about 1 inch (2.5 cm). Trim excess to about 1½ inches (3 cm). This will be hidden when you line the purse.

*Making the shoulder strap*

**16.** Pin the center of each remaining eight cords to your knotting board. Place them side by side. The ends will hang over the top and bottom of your board.

**17.** Tie a square knot with the four cords on the left, directly under the T-pins. Tie another square knot with the four cords on the right. This is the first row.

### FINISHED SIZE
12 x 12 inches (30 x 30 cm)

### KNOTS USED
Lark's head, square, double half hitch, half hitch

### MATERIALS
237 yards of 4mm braided polypropylene macramé cord:
- 30 cords cut 6 yards (5.4 m) each for the shoulder bag body
- 1 cord cut 1 yard (90 cm) for the holding cord
- 8 cords cut 7 yards (6.3 m) each for the shoulder strap

### TOOLS
Measuring tape
Scissors
Macramé work board
T-pins
Crochet hook #6 or G

**18.** Use the center four cords (omit the first and last two cords) and make one square knot. This is the second row. Tie your knots firmly, and keep them horizontal and even.

**19.** Continue making alternating square knots for 17 inches (42 cm). Make sure your last row has just one square knot.

**20.** Turn board around and work the other side of the strap in the same way. Knot for 17 inches (42 cm).

*Attaching the strap to the body of the bag*

**21.** Lay the body of the bag out flat on a table, with the wrong side facing up. Fold the (holding cord) end up 11 inches (27.5 cm). Make sure both sides are even before you start to attach the strap.

**22.** Number your strap cords from left to right 1 through 8. Position the shoulder strap on the left side of the bag, between the front and back of the body.

**23.** From the start of your double hitched edge, count down to the seventh side loop. Now, using your crochet hook, pull strap cords 1 and 2 through the seventh side loop on the back of the body from the outside in.

**24.** Tie a square knot with strap cords 1, 2, 3, and 4.

**25.** Using your crochet hook, pull strap cords 7 and 8 through the first side loop on the front of the body. Pull the cords from the outside in.

**26.** Tie a square knot with strap cords 5, 6, 7, and 8. The two square knots you just tied make the first row of our strap attachment.

**27.** For the next row, we'll make a single square knot with cords 3, 4, 5, and 6.

*Continue attaching the strap to the bag in this manner until you reach the fold at the bottom. Make sure your last row has two square knots.*

**28.** Pull your strap cords through the bottom loops, and make two more square knots on the inside of the bag. Turn the piece inside out.

**29.** Use an overhand knot to secure your ends. Trim the ends, leaving about an inch (2.5 cm) extra.

**30.** Repeat steps 21–29 to attach the other side of the strap to the bag.

**31.** Using your crochet hook, pull the holding cord (used in the first row) through the straps knots. Secure the ends with overhand knots and trim.

**OPTIONAL:** *Line your Blue Beauty Shoulder Bag with an attractive fabric. Sew a piece of hook-and-loop tape to the flap and the front of the purse for extra security.*

# MAPLE SUGAR NECKLACE

*The crisp symmetry of waxed linen knotting combined with the warmth of wooden beads creates this sweet necklace.*

DESIGNER: **ELAINE LIEBERMAN**

## FINISHED LENGTH

Approximately 16 inches
(40 cm) long

## KNOTS USED

Square, double half hitch,
half hitch, overhand

## MATERIALS

7-ply natural color waxed linen
- 2 cords cut 13 feet (3.9 m)
- 2 cords cut 7 feet (2 m)
- 6 cords cut 5 feet (150 cm)

2 jump rings (4mm)

16 maple oval beads
   (6mm x 9mm)

2 flat maple beads (10mm wide)

1 barrel clasp

## TOOLS

Measuring tape
Scissors
Macramé work board
T-pins
Chain-nose pliers
Clear-drying glue

## INSTRUCTIONS

**1.** String one 7-foot (2 m) cord and one 13-foot (3.9 m) cord through a jump ring to their center points. Secure your work (jump ring and cords) to your knotting board, using a T-pin. You now have four working cords—two are 3½ feet (1 m) long, and two are 6½ feet (1.9 m) long.

**2.** Using the two short working cords as your anchors, make a square knot sennit approximately 8 inches (20 cm) long.

**3.** String one oval, one flat, and one more oval bead onto your anchor cords.

**4.** Float the knotting cords around the beads, and make eight more square knots.

**5.** Repeat steps 1–4 to make the other side.

**6.** Fold two of the 5-foot (150 cm) cords in half. Secure one side of each cord to your board, keeping them close together. One of these cords will be your knot-bearer, and one will be your knotter.

**7.** Place the center of your knotting cord behind the center of the knot bearer, and make a double half hitch. Make another double half hitch with the other side of the knotting cord.

**8.** Mount the four cords from one of your square knot sennits onto the knot-bearer, using double half hitches.

**9.** Attach two more of the 5-foot (150 cm) cords, just as you did in step 7.

**10.** Repeat step 8 with the cords from the other square knot.

**11.** Repeat step 9. (You should now have 18 working cords, including both ends of your knot-bearer.)

**12.** Your remaining 5-foot cord will now be added as the new knot-bearer. Starting near the center point of the knot-bearer, attach each of the 18 cords with double half hitches. (You should now have 20 working cords—let's number them 1–20, from left to right.)

**13.** Make a row of five square knots, with four cords each.

**14.** With cord 2, tie a single half hitch around cord 1.

**15.** With cord 1, tie a single half hitch around cord 2.

**16.** Repeat step 14.

**17.** Repeat step 15.

**18.** Make two square knots with cords 3–6.

**19.** Make one square knot with cords 7–10.

**20.** Make one square knot with cords 11–14.

**21.** Make two square knots with cords 15–18.

**22.** Repeat steps 14–17, using cords 19 and 20.

**23.** Make one square knot with cords 9–12.

**24.** String one oval bead onto cords: 1, 4, 7, 14, 17, and 20.

**25.** Using cords 10 and 11 as your knot-bearers, make rows of diagonal double half hitches in either direction.

**26.** Repeat step 25. (Now, we'll create a diamond of square knots.)

**27.** Repeat step 23.

**28.** Repeat step 19.

**29.** Make one square knot with cords 5–8.

**30.** Make one square knot with cords 3–6. (Each of the last three square knots you made should be a little lower than the one before it.)

**31.** Repeat step 20.

**32.** Make one square knot with cords 13–16.

**33.** Make one square knot with cords 15–18.

**34.** Repeat step 29.

**35.** Repeat step 19.

**36.** Repeat step 32.

**37.** Repeat step 20.

**38.** Repeat step 23.

**39.** Using cord 1 as your knot-bearer, make a row of diagonal double half hitches with cords 2–10, towards the center.

**40.** Using cord 20 as your knot-bearer, make a row of diagonal double half hitches with cords 19–11, towards the center.

**41.** Repeat step 39.

**42.** Repeat step 40.

**43.** Repeat step 23.

**44.** Repeat step 24.

**45.** Repeat steps 14–22.

**46.** Repeat step 13.

**47.** Using cord 1 as knot-bearer, make a row of horizontal double half hitches from left to right, then back from right to left.

**48.** Using cords 1 and 5 as your knotting cords, and 2, 3, and 4 as your anchor cords, tie four square knots.

**49.** Use cord 5 to tie an overhand knot around the ends of the square knot you just made. Tighten with the knot at the back of the necklace.

**50.** Repeat steps 48 and 49 with cords 16–20.

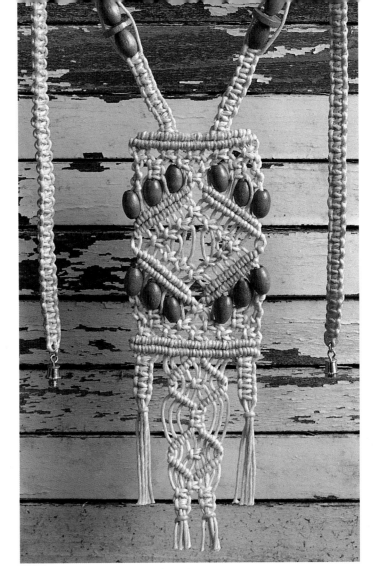

**51.** Using cords 10 and 11 as your knot-bearers, make rows of diagonal double half hitches to either side.

**52.** Make a square knot with cords 9–12.

**53.** Using cords 6 and 15 as knot-bearers, make rows of diagonal double half hitches toward the center.

**54.** Make two square knots with cords 9–12.

**55.** Repeat steps 51–53.

**56.** Make one square knot with cords 9–12.

**57.** Using cords 6 and 10 as your knotting cords, and 7, 8, and 9 as your anchor cords, tie two square knots.

**58.** Using cords 11 and 15 as your knotting cords, and 12, 13, and 14 as your anchor cords, tie two square knots.

**59.** Finish off these square knots as you did in step 49.

**60.** Trim the middle square knots' ends to about ½ inch (13mm).

**61.** Trim the outer ends so they are about ½ inch (13mm) shorter than the middle ones.

**62.** Apply a dab of glue to the overhand knots and the ends. Allow to dry.

**63.** Attach the clasp.

# MAGICAL MYSTERY MARKETING BAG

*There's really no mystery to it! It's hemp, it's cool, and it's the definitive answer to the "paper or plastic?" dilemma.*

DESIGNER: **ELAINE LIEBERMAN**

## FINISHED LENGTH

Approximately 23 inches (57.5 cm) long

## KNOTS USED

Lark's head knots, overhand, double half hitch, square

## MATERIALS

24 small wooden rings (you could also use plastic rings, or donut beads)

Hemp cord, 2mm
- 24 cords cut 12 feet (3.6 m) each
- 8 cords cut 11 feet (3.3 m) each

## TOOLS

Measuring tape

Scissors

Macramé work board 12 x 18 inches (30 x 45 cm)

T-pins

## INSTRUCTIONS

**1.** Mount the 24 cords to the rings with Lark's head knots.

**2.** Tie overhand knots in your cords, directly under the Lark's head knots.

**3.** Tie four of your remaining (strap) cords together with an overhand knot. Leave 4½ feet (135 cm) on one side of your knot, which will leave about 6½ feet (195 cm) on the other side.

**4.** String 12 of the rings onto the longer ends of the four cords.

**5.** Tie your four cords together with another overhand knot on the other side of the rings. Leave about 18 inches (45 cm) between the overhand knots.

**6.** Number your rings 1–12, from left-to-right.

**7.** Tie an overhand knot with the right-hand cord from ring 1 and the left-hand cord from ring 2. Make your knot about an inch (2.5 cm) from the straps.

**8.** Tie an overhand knot with the right-hand cord from ring 2 and the left-hand cord from ring 3.

**9.** Tie an overhand knot with the right-hand cord from ring 3 and the left-hand cord from ring 4.

*Continue with this overhand knotting pattern until you've used the left-hand cord on ring 12.*

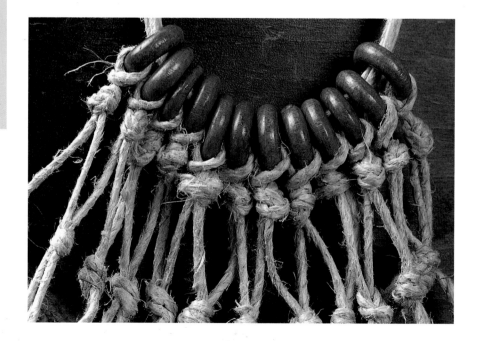

*Now, let's get the other side of the bag going.*

**10.** Repeat steps 3–9 with the remaining 12 rings and the remaining four cords.

**11.** Place one side of the bag on top of the other. Join the loose ends of the strap cords together on the left side with an overhand knot.

**12.** Repeat step 11 with the strap cords on the right side. (These cords will later be untied, so you don't have to worry about neatness.)

**13.** Place your rings around the length of your knotting board. You will be using both sides. (We will be working "in the round," so you might want to experiment with comfortable surfaces.)

**14.** Join the remaining unknotted cords together with overhand knots. You should now have both sides joined and one complete row of overhand knots.

**15.** Using an overhand knot, join the right-hand cord from one knot with the left-hand cord from the overhand knot to its right. Leave about ¾ inch (2 cm) between this knot and the one above it.

**16.** Repeat step 15 all the way around the bag, until you've made a second row.

**17.** Continue making rows of overhand knots in this manner. Make 16 rows.

**18.** Knot two more rows, but make them no more than ½ inch (13mm) from the previous one.

**19.** Position the bag so you have clear access to both sides along the bottom. Line the cords up so the two sides correspond. Find the left end cords from each side of the bag.

**20.** Join the two left end cords with an overhand knot.

**21.** Continue to tie the cords from each opposing side together with overhand knots, until you have completely connected the front and back of the bag.

**22.** Using the cord at the left-hand side of the bag as knot-bearer, make a row of horizontal double half hitches, from left to right, then back from right to left.

**23.** Tie your knot-bearer to the cord next to it using an overhand knot.

**24.** Trim your fringe to the desired length.

*Now, let's finish our straps.*

**25.** Untie the overhand knot that you made in step 11.

**26.** Make a square knot below each of the overhand knots with four cords.

**27.** Using the four center cords make one square knot.

**28.** Continue making an alternating square knot pattern for about 9 inches (22.5 cm). Make sure your last knot is one made with the center cords.

**29.** Repeat steps 25–28 on the other side of the strap.

*Now, we'll join the two ends of the straps together with square knots.*

**30.** Bring the ends of the straps together. Make sure all cords are straight.

**31.** Move the top two cords on each strap out of your way. Use the next two cords on each side to tie one square knot.

**32.** Use the two left cords from the square knot you just made, and the two cords you moved aside on the left, and make another square knot.

**33.** Use the two right cords from the square knot you made in step 31 and the two cords you moved aside on the right, and make another square knot.

**34.** Make one more square knot using the two inside cords from the previous two square knots.

**35.** Repeat steps 31–34 with the bottom four cords.

**36.** Using the left most cord of those you have just worked with as knot-bearer, make a row of three diagonal double half hitches, toward the center.

**37.** Repeat step 36 with the right cord.

**38.** Tie the two knot-bearers together with an overhand knot.

**39.** Trim each cord, leaving ½-inch (13mm) tails.

**40.** Repeat steps 36–39 on the other side of the strap.

# NECK RING CHOKER

*This bold choker features a variety of knots and techniques and shows off a stunning array of beads.*

DESIGNER: **LYNN SMYTHE**

## FINISHED LENGTH

16 inches (40 cm) around,
5 inches (12.5 cm) long

## KNOTS USED

Half hitch, Lark's head,
square, half knot,
double half hitch, overhand

## MATERIALS

20 yards (18 m) of 4-ply
   waxed linen:
- Approximately 5 yards
  (4.5 m) to cover neck ring*
- 19 cords cut 28 inches
  (70 cm) each

16-inch (40 cm) metal neck ring

8 two-hole 20mm x 8mm
   crescent-shaped beads,
   1 each of graduated colors

38 round 2mm copper beads

80 round 3mm copper beads

3 glass crow beads

2 brass barrel beads

## TOOLS

Tape measure

Scissors

Blunt end tapestry needle

Macramé work board

T-pins

Locking hemostats or pliers

Beading awl

Clear-drying glue
   or clear nail polish

*NOTE: *The first step in creating this choker is to completely cover the neck ring with half hitches. You'll find it easier if you start with an entire 10-yard (30 cm) spool of waxed linen, rather than cutting such a long piece.*

## INSTRUCTIONS

**1.** Fold the end of your cord, from the spool of waxed linen, over about an inch (2.5 cm) and place it on one end of the neck ring.

**2.** Begin half hitching. Be sure to cover both the folded end and the neck ring.

**3.** When you have made about 10 half hitches, trim what remains of the short end.

**4.** Continue half hitching to cover the neck ring. Keep your knotting dense and tight. Your cord will naturally spiral. Shape it by hand to keep it straight.

**5.** When you get to the end of the neck ring, cut the waxed linen from the spool, leaving a 6-inch (15 cm) tail.

**6.** Thread the tail onto the tapestry needle and work it back into the half hitches to secure. Cut the cord close to the knotting.

**7.** Fold the 19 cords in half and mount to the middle of the neck ring using Lark's head knots.

**8.** Secure your work to your knotting board with T-pins.

**9.** Number your cords from left to right, 1–38.

**10.** String a 3mm copper bead on cords 19 and 20, followed by a 2-hole crescent bead. Repeat until you have used all 8 crescent beads. Hold these beads in place temporarily with a pair of locking hemostats or pliers.

**11.** Tie a square knot with cords 1–6, using cords 3 and 4 as your anchor cords.

**12.** Tie a square knot with cords 7–12, using cords 9 and 10 as your anchor cords.

**13.** Tie a square knot with cords 13–18, using cords 15 and 16 as your anchor cords.

**14.** Pin cord 1 out of your way.

**15.** Make 10 half knots with cords 2–5, using cords 3 and 4 as your anchors. (This will create a natural twist.)

**16.** String one 3mm copper bead on cord 6.

**17.** Make eight half knots with cords 6–9.

**18.** String one 3mm copper bead on cord 13.

**19.** Make eight half knots with cords 10–13.

**20.** Make eight half knots with cords 14–17.

**21.** String five 3mm copper beads on cord 1.

**22.** Repeat step 16.

**23.** Repeat step 11.

**24.** Repeat step 12.

**25.** Repeat step 18.

**26.** String four 3mm copper beads on cord 18.

**27.** Repeat step 13.

**28.** Use cord 1 as knot-bearer, and make two rows of horizontal double half hitches, first from left to right, then back from right to left.

**29.** Tie one square knot with cords 1–5; (use cords 3 and 4 as anchors).

**30.** Tie one square knot with cords 6–9.

**31.** Tie one square knot with cords 10–13.

**32.** Tie one square knot with cords 14–18; (use cords 15 and 16 as anchors).

**33.** Tie one square knot with cords 7–12; (use cords 9 and 10 as anchors).

**34.** Repeat step 16.

**35.** Repeat step 11.

**36.** Repeat step 18.

**37.** Repeat step 13.

**38.** String one 3mm copper bead on cords 9 and 10.

**39.** Tie one square knot with cords 1–4.

**40.** Tie one square knot with cords 5–8.

**41.** Tie one square knot with cords 11–14.

**42.** Tie one square knot with cords 15–18.

**43.** Repeat step 33.

**44.** Repeat step 16.

**45.** Repeat step 11.

**46.** Repeat step 18.

**47.** Repeat step 13.

**48.** Repeat steps 29-32.

**49.** Make 10 half knots with cords 1–4.

**50.** Make 12 half knots with cords 5–8.

**51.** String two 3mm copper beads on cord 9 and two on cord 11.

**52.** String one crow bead onto cords 9, 10, and 11.

**53.** Repeat step 51.

**54.** Make 12 half knots with cords 12–15.

**55.** Make 12 half knots with cords 16–19.

**56.** Repeat steps 11,12, and 13.

*Now, we'll work on the second half of the necklace, using cords 21–38.*

**57.** Repeat steps 12–51.

**58.** Tie three square knots with cords 14–17.

**59.** Tie three square knots with cords 22–25.

**60.** String one 3mm copper bead on cord 19 and one on cord 20.

**61.** Make five square knots with cords 18–21.

**62.** String a brass barrel bead, a crow bead, and another brass barrel bead onto cords 19 and 20.

**63.** Make 12 alternating half hitches with cords 19 and 20. (First make a half hitch with cord 19 around 20, then 20 around 19—for a total of 12.) Repeat with cords 15 and 16, and with cords 23 and 24.

**64.** String one 2 mm copper bead on cord 1, and secure with an overhand knot. Use a T-pin or the beading awl to slide the knot down close to the copper bead. Cut the cord close to the knot.

**65.** Place a drop of clear-drying glue or clear nail polish on the knot, and let dry.

**66.** Repeat steps 64 and 65 with the rest of your cords.

# RAINBOW CARD CADDY

*This colorful and clever card caddy is made entirely from alternating diagonal double half hitches.*

DESIGNER: **JIM GENTRY**

## FINISHED LENGTH

Approximately 3 inches (7.5 cm) wide and 4 inches (10 cm) long

## KNOTS USED

Lark's head, overhand, diagonal double half hitch, square

## MATERIALS

Embroidery floss (five skeins of each color)

- Cut all cords 4 feet, 2 inches (125 cm) long
- 16 cords of red
- 16 cords of orange
- 16 cords of yellow
- 16 cords of green
- 16 cords of blue
- 16 cords of purple

**For the Card Caddy Cover:**

- 16 cords of green, blue and purple
- 20 cords of red, orange and yellow

Waxed Linen 3-ply natural color

- 1 cord cut 20 inches (50 cm)
- 1 cord cut 20 inches (50 cm) for the Card Caddy Cover

Round leather lace or braided cotton cord, 2mm

- 1 cord cut 36 inches (90 cm)

## TOOLS

Measuring tape

Scissors

Corrugated cardboard strips

- 1 strip cut 2⅝ inches (6.5 cm) wide and 10 inches (25 cm) long
- 1 strip cut 3 inches (7.5 cm) wide and 10 inches (25 cm) long
- 1 strip cut 3 inches (7.5 cm) wide and 10 inches (25 cm) long for the Card Caddy Cover

Heavy yarn needle

Cross-stitch needle

*We will double up our cords for this project (just as we did with the Best-Seller Bookmark). Therefore, when you see the term "cord" in the instructions, it refers to two strands of embroidery floss combined to make one. (Our 16 cords of red will become 8.) Keep in mind, too, that the number of the cord represents the position of the cord and this position never changes, although the actual cords do.*

## INSTRUCTIONS

**1.** Wrap one of the cords of waxed linen around the smaller piece of cardboard twice. Make a square knot to secure. Keep this cord about 3 inches (7.5 cm) from the top of the cardboard. Trim the ends close. This will be your holding cord.

*Now, we'll mount all of our working cords. We will find the center points of our cords and mount them with Lark's head knots. Follow the mounting order correctly; this is what creates our rainbow pattern.*

**2.** Starting at the left-hand side of the cardboard, mount two cords (remember that's actually four strands) of red, two cords of orange, two cords of yellow, two cords of green, two cords of blue, and two cords of purple.

**3.** Repeat step 2.

**4.** Turn the cardboard over and repeat step 2, twice. Now we're ready to begin our diagonal double half hitches.

**5.** Number the first red cords you mounted, from left to right, 1–4.

**6.** Using cord 1 as knot-bearer and cord 2 as your knotting cord, tie a diagonal double half hitch. (Hold the knot-bearer with your right hand and knot with your left.)

**7.** Using cord 3 as knot-bearer and cord 4 as your knotting cord, tie a diagonal double half hitch. (Holding your knot-bearer taut and diagonal will help ensure a uniform looking pattern.)

**8.** Using cord 3 as knot-bearer and cord 2 as your knotting cord, tie a diagonal double half hitch. (Hold the knot-bearer with your left hand and knot with your right.)

**9.** Repeat steps 6–8 with each group of four, all the way around. This will create your first two rows.

*Row one has two diagonal double half hitches going to the right. Row two has a single diagonal double half hitch going to the left. As you continue, remember that odd-numbered rows are knotted to the right, and even-numbered rows are knotted to the left.*

**10.** Continue knotting until you have 52 rows. (The pouch will be about 3½ inches [8.75 cm] long.)

**11.** Identify the first two and last two cords on the front and back of the pouch, and tie with very loose overhand knots.

**12.** Remove the cardboard and turn the pouch inside out.

**13.** Slip the pouch back onto the cardboard, so that the bottom of the pouch is even with the bottom of the cardboard.

**14.** Position the pouch so that the cords you identified in step 11 are in their original positions.

*Now, let's tie up the bottom of our card caddy.*

**15.** Tie a square knot with the first two cords on the front and the last two cords on the back.

**16.** Continue making square knots with each group of four cords (two from the front, and two from the back).

**17.** Trim the ends to about ¼ inch (6mm).

**18.** Remove the cardboard and turn the pouch right side out. Do this carefully.

*Now let's make the card caddy cover.*

**19.** Tie the second piece of waxed linen around the cardboard as described in step 1.

**20.** Repeat steps 2, 3, and 4. When you have finished mounting your last purple cords, mount the remaining two red, orange, and yellow cords. (This extra length is needed for the cover to fit over the pouch.)

**21.** Repeat steps 5–9.

**22.** Continue knotting until the cover is 1⅜ inches (1.25 cm) long.

**23.** Repeat steps 11–18.

*Finally, let's add our necklace cord.*

**24.** Thread your heavy yarn needle with one end of your round leather or braided cotton cord. Insert the needle through one corner of the card caddy cover, and gently pull the cord through.

**25.** Tie an overhand knot about an inch (2.5 cm) from the end of the cord.

**26.** Place the knotted end of the cord inside the pouch along the side fold. The knot should be about ½ inch (13mm) below the top edge of the pouch.

**27.** To secure the cord, use embroidery floss in the color of your choice and your cross-stitch needle, and make about 10 loop stitches around the cord. Stitch through the pouch side and around the cord. Stitch above the overhand knot.

**28.** Tie off your floss on the inside of the pouch and trim.

**29.** Repeat step 24 on the other side of the cover.

**30.** Repeat steps 25–28 on the other side of the pouch. (Make the necklace cord any length you desire.)

# HEART STOPPER COPPER RING

*What could be lovelier than a ring of double intertwining Josephine knots? Two. Make one of yourself and one for your sweetie.*

DESIGNER: **LINDA ROSE NALL**

**FINISHED SIZE**

Make to fit

**KNOTS USED**

Josephine

**MATERIALS**

24-gauge copper wire
- 9 pieces cut 7 inches (17.5 cm) each

**TOOLS**

Measuring tape

Cutting pliers

Needle-nose pliers

Ring mandrel or dowel

## INSTRUCTIONS

**1.** Divide wires into three groups of three. Number the groups 1, 2, and 3.

**2.** Make a Josephine knot with groups 1 and 2. Form your loops at the center points of each group. Work slowly and carefully.

**3.** Bring the ends of group 1 and 2 that are above the Josephine knot together.

**4.** Bring the ends of group 1 and 2 that are below the Josephine knot together.

**5.** Trim group 1 wires to about an inch (2.5 cm) and wrap around group 2. (Use needle-nose pliers to help hide the ends of the wires.)

*We now have one Josephine knot made from group 1 and 2. On either side of this knot, the ends of group 1 are wrapped around group 2, leaving group 2 wires sticking out on either side. One side of these (group 2) wires will be used to make a second Josephine knot. Let's call this side A. The other side of the (group 2) wires will be used to circle around and create the actual ring. Let's call this side B.*

**6.** Make a loop with side A.

**7.** Use group 3 wires to form another loop (at the center point) and weave it into the side A loop. This creates our second Josephine knot.

**8.** Wrap the ends of the group 3 wires around the existing wrapped area. This creates the wrapped middle of your ring. (Use your needle-nose pliers to bury the sharp ends.)

**9.** Wrap one of the sets of wires coming from the other side of the Josephine knot around the other. We now have just one set of wires on either side.

**10.** Wrap the ends around a ring mandrel (or dowel) to make the size you want.

**11.** Once you have the ring properly sized, wrap your excess wire around the existing wrapped areas. Trim your wires some if you want smaller wrappings. (Make sure all the ends are tucked safely into the wrappings and away from your finger.)

# PURPLE HEART PIN

*Here's an award-winner. Cavandoli is the wonderful technique of two-color double half hitching that lets you draw with knots.*

DESIGNER: **ROXY MOSTELLER**

*The primary color is the color of the working cords (purple) and is revealed with horizontal double half hitches. The accent colors (lavender and turquoise) are used as the knot-bearers, but are hidden by the purple half hitching. These accent colors are revealed (and the purple is hidden) with vertical double half hitches around the purple working cords.*

## INSTRUCTIONS

**1.** Secure the 18-inch (45 cm) purple cord to your knotting board with pins. This is your holding cord.

**2.** Mount the 9 purple cords by folding them in half and attaching with horizontal double half hitches.

**3.** Mount the 15-inch (37.5 cm) purple cord on the right side of your holding cord, using horizontal double half hitches, but this time let about 13 inches (32.5 cm) hang below the holding cord. This is your first (mounting) row.

**4.** You now have 19 working cords. Working from right to left, and using your 13-inch (32.5 cm) cord as knot-bearer, make a row of horizontal double half hitches. This is your second row.

**5.** For rows 3–20, follow the graph on page 106. Switch knot-bearers, as indicated, to reveal your turquoise and lavender accent colors. Keep your rows even and your knotting tight. (Remember, each accent color is a vertical double half hitch, and each graph square equals one complete double half hitch.)

*Now, let's finish the pin.*

**6.** Using your crochet hook, weave the ends of your knot-bearers and holding cord through the back side of two or three knots, and trim.

**7.** Trim the working cord ends to about 1¼ inches (3 cm).

**8.** Sew on the seed beads in the shape of an arrow.

**9.** Lightly dab the back of the pin with glue. Use glue sparingly.

**10.** Fold all the cord ends to the back of the pin and smooth down.

**11.** Place the square of waxed paper over the back and weight it down until the glue is dry.

**12.** Trim the felt square to fit the back of the pin, but make sure it doesn't show from the front.

## FINISHED SIZE
1½ inches (3.75 cm) square, excluding tassel

## KNOTS USED
Horizontal and vertical double half hitch, square

## MATERIALS
Size 10 crochet thread in three colors (purple, lavender, and turquoise are used)

**Purple**
- 1 cord cut 18 inches (45 cm)
- 9 cords cut 1½ yards (1.35 m) each
- 1 cord cut 15 inches (37.5 cm)

**For the Tassel**
- 1 cord cut 35 inches (87.5 cm)
- 2 cords cut 10 inches (25 cm) each

**Turquoise**
- 1 cord cut 2 yards (1.8 m)

**Lavender**
- 1 cord cut 2 yards (1.8 m)

Felt (to match primary color) 1⅝ inches (4 cm) square

1 bar pin 1 inch (2.5 cm) long

9 turquoise seed beads

## TOOLS
Measuring tape

Scissors

Macramé work board

Straight pins (ball cap are easiest on your fingers)

Size 10 or 11 crochet hook

Needle and matching thread (optional)

White or fabric glue

Square of waxed paper, 5 inches (12.5 cm)

Square of cardboard, 2 inches (5 cm)

**13.** Make two slits in the felt to slide the bar pin through. The bar pin should be slightly above the middle of the square.

**14.** Apply glue lightly to the back of the felt and the bar pin. Place the felt and pin against the back of the knotting, and weight it down until the glue is dry. (You may sew the felt square to the pin if you prefer.)

*To make the tassel:*

**15.** Wrap the 35-inch (87.5 cm) cord around the 2-inch (5 cm) piece of cardboard eight times.

**16.** Using a 10-inch (25 cm) cord, tie the wrapped cords together at the top of the cardboard with a square knot.

**17.** Cut the wrapped cords at the other end and discard the cardboard.

**18.** With another 10-inch (25 cm) cord, tie a square knot around all the cords about ¼ inch (6mm) from the top. Smooth the ends down, and trim even with the ends of the tassel.

**19.** Attach tassel to the bottom corner of the pin with the two ends of the square knot you made in step 16.

**20.** Using your crochet hook, bring the ends to the back of the pin and tie. Trim and dab with glue to secure.

|  | 1 | 2 | 3 | 4 | 5 | 6 | 7 | 8 | 9 | 10 | 11 | 12 | 13 | 14 | 15 | 16 | 17 | 18 | 19 |  |
|---|---|---|---|---|---|---|---|---|---|---|---|---|---|---|---|---|---|---|---|---|
| 1→ | P | P | P | P | P | P | P | P | P | P | P | P | P | P | P | P | P | P | P | ←2 |
| 3→ | P | P | P | P | P | P | P | P | P | P | T | P | T | P | T | P | P | P | P | |
| | P | P | P | P | P | P | P | P | P | T | L | L | L | L | L | T | P | P | P | ←4 |
| 5→ | P | P | P | P | P | P | P | P | T | L | L | L | L | L | L | L | T | P | P | |
| | P | P | P | P | P | P | P | P | L | L | T | L | T | L | L | L | P | P | P | ←6 |
| 7→ | P | P | P | P | P | P | P | T | L | L | P | P | P | T | L | L | L | T | P | |
| | P | P | P | P | P | P | P | P | L | T | P | P | P | P | T | L | L | P | P | ←8 |
| 9→ | P | P | P | T | P | T | P | T | L | L | P | P | P | P | P | L | L | T | P | |
| | P | P | T | L | L | L | L | L | L | T | P | P | P | P | P | T | L | P | P | ←10 |
| 11→ | P | T | L | L | L | L | T | L | T | T | P | P | P | P | P | L | L | T | P | |
| | P | P | L | L | T | P | P | P | P | P | P | P | P | P | P | T | L | P | P | ←12 |
| 13→ | P | T | L | L | L | P | P | P | P | P | P | P | P | P | P | L | L | T | P | |
| | P | P | L | L | T | P | P | P | P | P | P | P | P | P | P | T | L | P | P | ←14 |
| 15→ | P | T | L | L | L | T | P | P | P | P | P | P | P | P | P | L | L | T | P | |
| | P | P | T | L | L | L | T | P | P | P | P | P | P | P | P | T | L | P | P | ←16 |
| 17→ | P | P | P | T | L | L | L | L | T | L | T | L | T | L | T | T | L | T | P | |
| | P | P | P | P | P | L | L | L | L | L | L | L | L | L | L | L | L | P | P | ←18 |
| 19→ | P | P | P | P | P | T | P | T | P | T | P | T | P | T | P | T | P | T | P | |
| | P | P | P | P | P | P | P | P | P | P | P | P | P | P | P | P | P | P | P | ←20 |

# MEET THE DESIGNERS

### IRMA BIEGELMAN

Irma Biegelman has been an avid crafter and teacher for 25 years. She has taught macramé to senior citizens on Long Island for the past 17 years. Her fine knotted work is available through her business, Modern Macramé, in Merrick, New York.

### MARISANDE FISHER

Marisande Fisher studied fiber arts at the University of Washington. She creates beautiful hand-dyed hemp twine, available through her business, Radiant Hemp. Contact her at Marisand@scn.org.

### JIM GENTRY

Jim Gentry has more than 25 years' experience in fiber arts. He is self-taught in macramé and has contributed his talents to public schools, public television and a veritable plethora of workshops. Jim resides in Gatlinburg, Tennessee. He may be contacted at JAAG1@prodigy.net.

### JENNIFER M. LAKE

Jennifer Lake of Jenn's Gems creates unique hemp and gemstone jewelry, beaded watches, ankle bells, hair-wraps, and intriguing necessities. Visit her at www.jennsgems.com.

### ELAINE LIEBERMAN

Elaine Lieberman creates macramé jewelry, wall hangings, and other unique knotted pieces. She teaches classes in macramé and jewelry making, and sells her work through her business, Handcrafted by Elaine. She's online at www.elainecraft.com.

### BERNADETTE MAHFOOD

Bernadette Mahfood has been combining her two loves—glass and knotting—for the past five years, through her Winona, Minnesota studio, Hot Flash Designs. She teaches knotted fiber jewelry making and glass techniques at her studio and at workshops around the country.

### ROXY MOSTELLER

Roxy Mosteller is a fiber and mixed-media artist based in Hartsville, South Carolina. She has taught off-loom textile techniques in a variety of settings and has been active in non-profit visual arts organizations for over 20 years. She received a BA in Fine Arts from Coker College in 1991.

### LINDA ROSE NALL

Linda Rose Nall, of Silver Rose Rhapsodies, has been creating wire jewelry since 1989. She specializes in wire-wrapped earrings with beads and stones, stained glass jewelry, and functional items. Her works are available at fine galleries and shops throughout Western North Carolina and beyond. Visit her at her website: www.brwm.org/rhapsodies.

### JANE OLSON

Jane Olson creates unusual knotted fiber jewelry using linen and cotton thread, stones, fossils, and a variety of beads. Jane is a former president of Beadesigner International, and the founder of the Baton Rouge Bead Society.

### JOH RICCI

Joh Ricci lives with her husband on their farm in New Oxford, Pennsylvania, where she creates her sculptural fiber pieces and hand-crafted jewelry through her business, Earthwalk Studios.

### DR. KEITH RUSSELL

Dr. Keith Russell is a Design and Communication philosopher, currently teaching at the University of Newcastle in Australia. He is a widely published poet, reviewer, and literary critic. Dr. Russell has been making macramé pieces for over 25 years.

### LYNN SMYTHE

Lynn Smythe is a bead and fiber "junkie" residing in southeast Florida, where she feeds her addiction by writing articles and teaching classes on beading and fiber art techniques. She is the founder of the Palm Beach Bead Society. Further evidence of her affliction can be seen on her Dolphin Crafts website at: members.aol.com/dlphcrft/index.htm.

### SANDY SWIRNOFF

Sandy Swirnoff, a former social worker serving abused women, closed her therapy practice to open her jewelry-making studio. Sandy designs and creates necklaces that combine macramé, flame-worked glass, beads, turquoise, amber, pearls, and other semiprecious stones. This jewelry artist divides her time between Minneapolis and San Diego.

### PAT THIBODEAUX

Pat Thibodeaux is a gardener who raises plants and cut flowers to sell in the summer. In winter, she makes baskets and beautiful bead and macramé jewelry. She also runs a guest apartment on the Toe River, north of Asheville, North Carolina.

### TRAVIS WALDRON

Travis Waldron, is a nautical knotter and crafter, and she creates hand-dyed natural fabrics, original wall quilts, unique gourd vessels, found-object jewelry, and painted glassware.

# GLOSSARY

**ANCHOR CORD:** (*A.K.A. filler and core*) The cords around which knots are tied. This term is used when referring to square knotting.

**BUTTERFLY BOBBIN:** A method of wrapping excess lengths of cord into manageable bundles.

**CAVANDOLI:** A creative knotting technique made entirely from horizontal and vertical double half hitches. Also referred to as *picture macramé* and *knotted tapestry*.

**DIAGONAL DOUBLE HALF HITCH:** A double half hitch tied over a diagonal knot-bearer.

**DOUBLE HALF HITCH:** (*A.K.A. Clove Hitch*) To loop a cord twice around a knot-bearer.

**FLOATING CORDS:** Cords that are unknotted and hang loose.

**GATHERING KNOT:** A knot used to draw together multiple cords into a single group.

**HALF HITCH:** (*A.K.A. simple knot, buttonhole loop*) A single loop tied around a knot-bearer. A continuous sennit of half hitches creates a spiral or corkscrew effect.

**HOLDING CORD:** The initial knot-bearer cord.

**HORIZONTAL DOUBLE HALF HITCH:** A double half hitch tied over a horizontal knot-bearer.

**JOSEPHINE KNOT:** (*A.K.A. Carrick bend*) A flat, decorative knot formed by two (or multiples of two) intertwined cords.

**KNOT-BEARER:** The cord(s) on which knots are tied. This term is used when referring to double half hitching.

**KNOTTING CORD:** The cord(s) with which knots are tied.

**LARK'S HEAD KNOT:** Knotting cords are typically mounted with this knot.

**MACRAMÉ WORK BOARD:** An appropriate surface used to secure works-in-progress.

**OVERHAND KNOT:** A looped knot often used to secure beads or finish the end of a single cord. It can be made with multiple cords.

**PICOT:** A decorative loop most often used for ornamental mounting or for making edges and borders.

**REVERSE DOUBLE HALF HITCH:** To loop a cord twice around a knot-bearer with the second loop in the direction opposite from the first.

**ROW:** A series of knots made next to each other in a straight line.

**SENNIT:** A length of continuously knotted cord.

**SQUARE KNOT:** Two half knots tied over anchor or filler cords. The number of cords varies.

**T-PINS:** Metal pins shaped like the letter T, used to keep knotting secured to a work board.

**VERTICAL DOUBLE HALF HITCH:** A double half hitch tied over a vertical knot-bearer.

**TWISTED SENNIT:** A length of continuous half knots.

# SUPPLIERS AND RESOURCES

Your local craft and jewelry supply stores carry all the materials needed for creating wonderful macramé jewelry and accessories. Below are some additional suppliers you may wish to consider.

**FOR CORD**

ROYALWOOD LTD.
517 Woodville Road
Mansfield, Ohio 44907
800-526-1618
www.bright.net/-roylwood/

THE OHIO HEMPERY, INC
P.O. Box 18
Guysville, OH 45735
800-BUY-HEMP

**FOR HAND-DYED HEMP**

RADIANT HEMP
Marisande Fisher
P.O. Box 75068
Seattle, WA 98125
Email: marisand@scn.org

**FOR TRADITIONAL POLYPROPYLENE CORD**

PEPPERELL BRAIDING COMPANY
P.O. Box 1487
Pepperell, MA 01463
800-343-8114
www.pepperell.com

**FOR COTTON CARPET THREAD**

EDGEMONT YARN SERVICE, INC.
P.O. Box 205
Washington, KY 41096
800-466-5977

**FOR WIRE**

ARTISTIC WIRE LTD.
1210 Harrison Avenue
LaGrange Park, IL 60526
(630) 530-7567
www.artisticwire.com

**FOR BEADS AND GENERAL JEWELRY SUPPLY**

J. BLUNDELL & SONS LTD.
199 Wardour Street
London W1V 4Jn
England
TEL 0207 437 4746
FAX 0207 734 0273
www.jblundell.co.uk

CHEVRON TRADING POST & BEAD CO.
40 N. Lexington Avenue
Asheville, NC 28801
(828) 236-2323
www.chevron-bead.com

DOLPHIN CRAFTS
Lynn Smythe
5416 Cleveland Road
Delray Beach, FL 33484-4276
(561) 496-7673
members.aol.com/dlphcrft/index.htm

LEICESTER THREAD & TRIMMING
107 Barkby Road
Leicester LE4 9LG
England
TEL 0116 276 5858
FAX 0116 246 0451

MUNRO'S
3954 West 12 Mile Road
Berkley, MI 48072
(248) 544-1590

RINGS & THINGS
P.O. Box 450
Spokane, WA 99210-0450
800-366-2156
www.Rings-Things.com

**FOR MACRAMÉ WORK BOARDS**

SAX Arts & Crafts
P.O. Box 51710
New Berlin, WI 53151
800-558-6696

# INDEX